Slave No More

"I've known Paul for many years, and this book represents the heart of my friend. It is a fantastic look into the core values and principles that lead to a life worth living. It smashes limiting beliefs and will help the reader fulfill their God-given potential and purpose. Obstacles, problems, setbacks, they get turned into opportunities, possibilities, and motivation."

—**Jimmy Page**, Speaker, and Author of many books including *One Word, Wisdom Walks,* and *True Competitor*

"Slave No More has charted the course with a collection of Underground Railroad stories to lead us toward freedom from our limiting thoughts. Page after page, the voices that shout "failure!" are quieted as you realize the power and potential that's within you. These stories are timeless and compelling in the truth they tell of freedoms that every human should journey to claim."

—**Kierra Henderson,** Creator, Beloved Mama
Founder, I Am Mama

"What will surprise many is how simply Paul identifies an unmistakable oversight in our psyche through story. One that reaches everyone, at every place in their lives. In a time when so much around us is chaotic, the 48 hours Bobby spends with Mr. J imparts a sense of controlled liberation and freedom from our self-induced chains. *Slave No More* is an essential, modern parable for those ready to pursue their purpose."

—**Ty Newell,** President, Outreach America

"Phenomenal story lines! As a black woman, I can see my family in this book. As a businesswoman, I can see my colleagues in this book. As an entrepreneur, I can see my clients in this book. There is a takeaway for everyone; a place to reflect, a place to learn, a place to grow."

—**Juanika Cuthbertson**, Founder, Ladypreneur® Academy

"In this book *Slave No More*, you will find that we all have a purpose, regardless of race or background. And this purpose is rarely discovered or achieved alone."

—**Travis Jones**, Lead Pastor, Motivation Church

"This book is timely and timeless at the same time, a book for today and a book for the ages. Paul masterfully illustrates through stories how a simple mind shift can create victory and freedom that we all desire."

—**Tim May**, Philanthropist

SLAVE NO MORE

CONQUERING THE MASTER WITHIN

PAUL A. HENDERSON

NEW YORK

LONDON • NASHVILLE • MELBOURNE • VANCOUVER

SLAVE NO MORE

Conquering the Master Within

Published in New York, New York, by Morgan James Publishing. Morgan James is a trademark of Morgan James, LLC. www.MorganJamesPublishing.com

Proudly distributed by Ingram Publisher Services.

Morgan James BOGO™

A **FREE** ebook edition is available for you or a friend with the purchase of this print book.

CLEARLY SIGN YOUR NAME ABOVE

Instructions to claim your free ebook edition:
1. Visit MorganJamesBOGO.com
2. Sign your name CLEARLY in the space above
3. Complete the form and submit a photo of this entire page
4. You or your friend can download the ebook to your preferred device

ISBN 9781631955945 paperback
ISBN 9781631955952 ebook
Library of Congress Control Number:
2021936027

Cover Concept by:
Kierra Henderson

Cover and Interior Design by:
Chris Treccani
www.3dogcreative.net

Author Photo by:
DeAudrea 'Sha' Rich

Interior Illustrations by:
Michael Stock

Morgan James is a proud partner of Habitat for Humanity Peninsula and Greater Williamsburg. Partners in building since 2006.

Get involved today! Visit MorganJamesPublishing.com/giving-back

To Patricia McGowan.
She is the teacher who saw more in me
than I saw in myself.

Acknowledgments

I want to acknowledge all of you who helped bring this book concept to life. Joe and Reva Dugger, Jewell Booker, Nolan Wilson, Emmett Bailey, and Randall Ward, thank you for sharing your personal stories of overcoming that helped me develop the manuscript's characters.

Gerri Semien, thank you for teaching about the different functions of garden hoses and fire hoses. Your explanation gave me a better understanding and helped bring a concept to life.

Marques Ruffin, thank you for reading my manuscript and offering your feedback. More than that, thank you for being a friend.

Bruce Vann, Tim May, Travis Jones, Johnny Shelton, Ty Newell, Amy Foley, Juanika Cuthbertson, Jimmy Page, and Bryan Berry, thank you for investing your time in reading my manuscript, offering feedback, and encouraging me to stay in the pursuit of my calling.

Michael Stock, thank you for bringing dimension to the concepts through your brilliant artwork. Even more, thank you for coming into my life when I was a twenty-year-old college student-athlete. You saw the best in me and gave me an opportunity to walk in my purpose.

Lynn Thompson, I could not have completed this book without you. Thank you for your editing expertise, your patience as I grow as a writer, and for welcoming my family of six into your world. Your guidance throughout this process has been invaluable.

Thank you, David Hancock and team at Morgan James Publishing for sharing the vision for my manuscript and accepting it for publication. Your support is greatly appreciated.

My parents, Steve and Sonya Henderson, thank you for all that you put into me. My brothers, Tim, Philip, Daniel, Josh, and Chris, thank you for your words for encouragement along the way.

My boys, PJ, Joey, David, and Noah, thank you for being you. Thank you for being such incredible blessings in my life and for giving me more reasons to live. I am proud of each of you, and I am eager to see you fulfill your God-given potential.

My beloved wife, Kierra, thank you for walking each step with me. This book project began during my job search in 2017, and you have been with me to the completion. Blessing my life with your encouragement, listening ear, and willingness to be present, I am beyond excited to live the rest of our lives together, fulfilling our purpose.

And to the One who showed me through His Word how to be a Slave No More, thank You.

Foreword

About ten years ago, while my wife and I were active in our local church, our sons, in their early teens and both heavily involved in athletics, had not yet connected with the youth pastor at the church. Schedules for practices, games, and team events often clashed with youth group events. When I discovered a local representative for the Fellowship of Christian Athletes who worked with my son's high school, I sought him out. After meeting Paul Henderson, I immediately wanted him to connect with my boys. I observed Paul develop friendships with a number of the athletes from the local high schools and build mentor-like relationships with numerous kids. I also watched as Paul dealt with the hurdles faced by guys in his position. Paul had to self-fund his activities, and that was a tough time economically. Many folks who wanted to contribute to his outreach were losing their jobs, and Paul had his own family to support. It was hard for me to see that ultimately, he had to leave his position with the FCA for another industry. However, Paul has never stopped influencing people and shaping lives. My wife and I have loved watching as he and his wife Kierra are building their beautiful family.

When Paul mentioned this book to me and asked me to read it, he only told me the title and just a summary of what he had written. I didn't know what to expect, but I was anxious to read it. Although it took me a little longer to get to it than I had planned, I read it three times in a matter of a couple of days.

Paul's message in *Slave No More* is a beautiful lesson to let go of the things in your past that may prevent you from becoming what you're meant to be.

In my own life, a former boss laughed at me for wanting to start my investment advisory firm. I've lost count of how many times I heard potential clients say that I wasn't good enough or that I was too small of a firm to handle large accounts. The number of times I let those remarks derail my goals is also a number I can't count. So, I learned to listen to the right voices. I made myself nurture the positive. Twenty-eight years into my career I faced a moment in my life where I questioned once again whether I was good enough. As I sought advice from the mentors I trusted, I realized it was time to pursue another life calling. When I was hindered once more, this time by a medical battle that I came very close to losing, the years of having learned to focus on the right voices became even more crucial.

In his inspirational book, Paul reminds us to take time to listen to the valuable stories of mentors. It's a subtle push to let the reader know that everyone faces hurdles and that the choice of what to do each time is yours to make.

Paul will be a positive influence in many lives. His boys are lucky to have him as a role model and I look forward to watching how Paul continues to nurture the positive seeds that will lead to thousands of impacted lives.

Bryan Berry, CFO Synapse, LLC

Preface

The inspiration for this book comes from a variety of life experiences—personal and observed. I have often witnessed people's tendency to hold their past in higher regard than their future, which begs the question, "Why?" We are alive in the present with our whole future ahead of us, so why do we allow the past to control us today?

Enter *Slave No More*. The whole idea is to encourage the reader that being bound to their past is an option. Over the years, personal acquaintances have shared their stories with me and how they overcame adverse life circumstances. I wonder what separates Person A, the overcomer, from Person B, the bound one. Is there much difference? Or can we narrow it down to a mindset?

This book has been a few years in the writing, and in the process, I have learned more about how to free myself from limiting thoughts. As you follow a young man's steps and lessons along the way, you will discover the power and effectiveness of having a strong vision to guide you through challenges. By the time you finish reading the book, I imagine that you will be ready to live with a sense of purpose, of being a slave no more.

Paul A. Henderson
Richmond, VA

CHAPTER 1

Bobby was frustrated. Another evening with another incomplete project looming over his head. Sitting at the small dining room table in his apartment, he stared at the instructions to what he had convinced himself was an endless task. The scattered pieces of the model train across the entire table were a depiction of his thoughts. His life felt derailed. The last thing he wanted to be doing on a Friday night in December was putting together any work project. *Why does this keep happening to me? Will I ever be able to finish anything that I start?* As he questioned himself, Bobby began replaying the list of incomplete tasks and assignments that burned in his memory of twenty-five years. The seventh-grade science fair project. The speech that he had tried to recite in front of his Social Studies class in eleventh grade. His senior term paper. He always experienced two common elements in every situation: He started strong, and he had trouble finishing.

Bobby interrupted his inner bully rant when Eric, his longtime friend, and new roommate, walked into the room. The look of frustration on Bobby's face was all too familiar to Eric.

Bobby and Eric had been friends since their freshman year in college, so Eric could always tell if there was something wrong with his friend. Their friendship continued into their young adult years when they recently started to share the apartment. Eric looked compassionately at the disarray on the table.

"Hey, what's up, Bobby? It looks like you're upset about something," Eric said.

Great. This is just what I need. I am already frustrated with this impossible project, and now I have to entertain Mr. Can-Do-No-Wrong? Yeah, he's successful now. Does he realize that I know that this was not always his case? I remember his struggles, and I remember his failures. "Eric, you know how it goes. You've heard it all before, we don't need to talk about it." *When will he learn? I don't always need his advice. The longer he stands there, the longer it will take for me to focus on this project. I wish he would leave me alone.*

Eric could see that his friend was troubled, so he paused for a moment. Eric walked over to Bobby, placed his hand on his friend's shoulder, and said, "Come on, Bobby. How long have we been friends? Something's going on; let's talk about it. Let me treat you to dinner."

An astonished Bobby looked at Eric because this was not a regular occurrence. *Treat me to dinner? Well, I am hungry, and I could use a break. So, what do I have to lose?* Bobby agreed, so they grabbed their coats and headed to Eric's car.

On the drive to their favorite burger joint, Eric asked, "It looks like you're in the middle of a project. What are you frustrated about?"

Bobby took a deep breath and exhaled loudly with a groan. *I really don't want to go into the details with him, but then, he is treating me to dinner. I guess I owe it to him, and I'll give it a shot.* "At work, we have this group Christmas project to present to a local boys' home. We were each given a role, and somehow, mine is way out of my expertise. You know that I am not good at those do-it-yourself jobs. I've been putting it off, and now I only have five days left. When I think of all the things that I like about the holiday season, parties, shopping, and gift exchanges, I don't see how I can complete my part of the project. It's more than an uphill battle. I feel like I'm staring at an unconquerable wall. How can I complete this task and still enjoy what's left of the holiday season?"

"Well, did you let the group know that your task is out of your league?" Eric asked.

"No, I couldn't do that. The project has everyone so pumped, and I don't want to be 'that guy,' you know?"

Eric replied, "Bobby, I think I know what you mean. And I admit that in the past, I have jumped to conclusions rather than hear you out. I really want to be sure that I completely understand your point of view. So, if you don't mind, could you tell me a little more?"

"Come on, Eric; you know exactly what I mean. I don't want to put a damper on everyone's excitement or have excuses. Who wants to hear about it? I'm afraid of being seen as a slacker."

Eric knew that Bobby cared about what people thought of him, especially about his abilities; that fear had hindered him over the years they'd been friends. Eric reflected on what he'd been recently learning while applying his life lessons and how he could help his friend tap into his potential, too. For a moment, Eric was silent as he gathered his thoughts.

CHAPTER 2

While the young men settled into the booth to eat once the waiter delivered their food, Eric glanced at Bobby before biting his burger. He was genuinely concerned for his friend for more reasons than Bobby realized. Even though he was familiar with how Bobby's limiting thoughts predominated his approach to school, work, and life, Eric also knew that Bobby did not have to be dominated by those thoughts. *How can I help my friend? It would be easy for me to tell him to stop having a pity party, except that I remember recently being in a similar place.*

When Eric finished chewing, he asked, "Bobby, can I ask you a couple of questions?"

Bobby looked at Eric with a blank stare. *What have I gotten myself into now? Is there any way that I can say, 'No'? He's treating me to dinner, so I guess I have to cooperate.* After taking a long sip of his soda, Bobby said, "Sure. Go ahead."

Eric leaned back in his booth. Even though he knew where this conversation could go, people had often mistaken his good intentions for arrogance. His concern for Bobby was genuine, and he wanted to be sure to communicate so that Bobby would know that his friend was in his corner. "You said a couple of things in the last hour that grabbed my attention."

Bobby looked at Eric sitting across from him, and Eric paused, studying his friend. Bobby's inner bully jumped on the bandwagon. *What did I say this time? There I go again, running my mouth and giving someone a reason to form an opinion of me. When will I learn?* The longer he examined Eric, though, the more he realized that his friend cared.

Still, Eric hesitated, considering his words before speaking further. He leaned forward, grabbed his straw, and began to stir his soda, looking down at his plate full of cold fries with a burger that had one bite out of it. Then he leaned back again.

Bobby was beginning to relax and continued to eat his food while anticipating what Eric would share from his observations.

Finally, Eric continued cautiously. "Bobby, you were pretty hard on yourself. You talked about your lack of skill for the project and that you're concerned about people's opinion of you. More than that, though, my concern is that you let those thoughts dominate you."

With a mouth full of food, Bobby glanced at Eric. Looking away as he swallowed, Bobby almost choked. *Who does this guy think he is to say that I've let anything dominate me? Does he believe that now that he's successful in his busi-*

ness, he knows everything about life? Rather than speaking his mind, Bobby reluctantly asked, "What do you mean by that? Saying that I let those thoughts dominate me?"

Looking directly into Bobby's eyes, Eric calmly said, "Bobby, I'm your friend. We've known each other for seven years. Before I say more, you need to know that I am not judging you in any way. I can relate to what you're feeling in more ways than you probably know."

Becoming more intrigued, Bobby nodded in agreement, urging Eric to continue.

"Bobby, you know that I've started my own business, and I already see some real success. You've been there from the beginning. Remember how much excitement I had at first? I didn't show it, so you may not realize that I've also dealt with a lot of doubt. I've wanted to quit more times than I can count."

Bobby nodded slowly, his eyes opening wider.

"Well, along the way, during the more discouraging days, I found myself replaying my failures." Eric paused, then continued. "Whether it was not living up to my potential when we played football in college or getting Cs in classes where I should have gotten As, I often found that I was living in my past and being dominated by it. You could say that I was a slave to my failures."

Bobby gave Eric a look of disgust. "A slave?" Bobby asked.

"Yes, a slave," Eric responded.

Bobby could not believe that Eric would relate anything that he was going through to being a slave. "Don't you think that's a little farfetched? I mean, come on."

Eric became aware that the restaurant would soon be closing due to the staff's anxious glances toward them. Their waiter had already dropped off the bill. Being thankful for a pause in their conversation, Eric pulled out his wallet and put cash on the table for their meals with a good tip. Eric and Bobby left the restaurant; in the car, they rode home in silence.

CHAPTER 3

When Bobby and Eric got back to their apartment, they took their coats off and sat at the dining room table. While Eric wanted to continue the conversation, he was worried about how Bobby was taking everything. *I hope that Bobby can see that I am genuinely concerned for him. I know that he's battling frustration with his project, and if I can just help him realize that I can relate, perhaps we can make some progress.*

Bobby, on the other hand, was becoming more intrigued and was ready for Eric to continue. The ride home from the restaurant had allowed Bobby to reflect on some of the thoughts his friend shared. *I can see that Eric is trying to help. But did he really compare my current state to some form of slavery? I wonder what he means by saying that he was a "slave to his failures."* Although some things were not easy to hear, he was beginning to see that Eric may be on to something.

"A slave?" Bobby asked again.

"Yes, Bobby," Eric responded, "a slave. If you think I'm crazy, pull out your phone, and look up the word 'slave.'"

Bobby dug into his pocket and grabbed his phone. He opened the web browser and typed in the word 'slave.' He read aloud the first two definitions. "Number one, 'a person held in servitude as the chattel of another.' And number two, 'one that is completely subservient to a dominant influence.' Number three—"

Eric stopped Bobby. "Okay. That second definition is what I'm referring to when I said, 'I was a slave to my failures.' Bobby, I had allowed my past to dominate me completely. My dad was never there, so I felt abandoned; my mom abused me verbally, and I experienced failure on the football field and in the classroom. I had a hard time breaking through to believing in myself. To be subservient means that I was allowing myself to submit to being controlled by my past. When I realized that was a choice I was making, I knew I had to come to terms with it."

Bobby sat quietly in deep thought as Eric's words resonated with him. *Eric and I have more in common than I realized. How am I just now finding out similarities with our paths when we've been friends for such a long time? Yet, he seems to have so much peace. How did he get to this point?*

Eric continued. "Bobby, let me tell you more about where I was at when I started my business and what happened when I reached out for help."

Bobby nodded. "Okay."

Eric leaned back in his chair and took a deep breath as he gathered his thoughts. "Bobby, remember how much I used to talk about having my own business?" Eric paused while Bobby was nodding. "What you don't know about are the thoughts that I battled at the beginning stages. You see, even with the big dream, I didn't know where to start. Doubt was overwhelming me. Like I mentioned earlier, my failures dominated my mind. I couldn't think of anyone who had run a successful business, so who would teach me? And I was raised by a single mom. I loved her, and I respect the fact that she raised my brother and me on her own. Deep down, though, I was searching for a father figure. Coach Johnson played that role for me when we were on his team. He was all the father I had. When our careers ended, and Coach moved on to another school, the relationship was not the same. And once again, I felt abandoned."

Bobby could relate to what Eric was sharing with him. And he was being drawn in by every word that Eric spoke because it seemed like even though they lived in parallel worlds, to this point, their journeys had taken them to different destinations.

"So, what did you do?" Bobby asked.

"Well, I decided to start networking," Eric responded. "You know the alumni association that the coaches told us about when we were preparing to graduate?"

"Sure," Bobby answered.

"Well," Eric continued, "I joined. Even though I wasn't sure what I was getting myself into, I attended the meetings with the hope of meeting someone who could help me. And then it happened."

Bobby's eyes were locked in on Eric with anticipation, ready to hear what happened.

Eric smiled and said, "I met Mr. J. Yep. Mr. J."

Bobby remembered Eric mentioning Mr. J's name from time to time, and he never thought much of it. Now he was eager to know. "Well, aren't you gonna tell me? Who is this Mr. J?"

"Sure," Eric answered. "Mr. J is a former football player, just like us. When I met him, I noticed that there was something different about him. First, I could tell that he was successful, even though he didn't flaunt it. He had a certain calmness about him. He took an interest in me. He willingly answered any questions I had about life without judging me. When he found out that I wanted to run my own business, rather than focus on what I needed, Mr. J pointed out the qualities he saw in me that he believed served me well."

"Wow," Bobby said, captivated.

Eric continued. "Yeah. He's the one who helped me get my insurance business up and going. And then, he began to provide me with valuable resources. I know you see me reading a lot, and you've noticed that I'm often lost in thought while I'm listening to something from my phone."

Bobby recalled seeing Eric with his earbuds in at their table, deep in thought, and taking notes. In those moments, Bobby always left Eric alone and never bothered to ask about the subject of his focused attention.

Eric continued. "Well, Mr. J recommended that I learn more about success principles by reading books and listening to podcasts," Eric's eyes grew bigger as he sat up straighter in his chair, "and I took him up on it. That decision has helped me tremendously. One of the things that he did that probably had the most impact on me was inviting me to spend a weekend with him at his home. Man, you talk about a weekend to remember! His hospitality was unlike anything I'd ever seen. His wife is great, and she served up fantastic meals for us all weekend. He took me around his hometown and introduced me to people with motivational stories that still inspire me to this day.

"When I left their home that weekend, I began to see my life in a new way because of Mr. J and everything I learned through him, his friends, and his wife. I began to rely more on my strengths rather than being overcome by my weaknesses. After a while, I was having some real success in my business. When I look back, I can see that it all started with me having a desire to be successful and then taking the initial step of finding a place to network with people who already had what I desired. From there, I was able to see the good in myself after someone took an interest without judging me. I listened to what he shared, and I applied that wisdom to my life and business."

Bobby sat there, reflecting on the last three to four years and what had changed for his friend, Eric. They both went to college. They both graduated. They both went right into the workforce, like most of their classmates. Then Eric began to do something outside of work that separated their success paths: he searched for and found a mentor. *How lucky is Eric to have found someone like Mr. J?*

I don't know if I would have the courage to approach someone successful—let alone seek out their mentorship.

"Eric, is there any way I could meet a guy like Mr. J?" Bobby asked.

"Well," Eric responded, "you're in luck. Mr. J has been looking for someone else to mentor. I mentioned your name and our history as friends and teammates, and he was intrigued by your story. If you're willing to take the time, he is available this weekend."

"This weekend?" a perplexed Bobby asked.

"Yep. This weekend. I already told Mr. J about you, and he told me to give you this message: 'If you are willing, I am ready.'"

Bobby was taken aback by how quickly everything was happening, and he thought about what was already on his plate. *I am so behind on my project; does it make sense for me to spend a weekend away from home? And for this Mr. J, why would he be looking for someone else to mentor? If he's already successful, what does he get out of it?*

Eric stood up, placed his hands on the table, and said, "Look, Bobby. I know you're behind on your work. So, here's what I'll offer. If you spend the weekend with Mr. J, I will help you with your project when you get home."

Bobby appreciated his friendship with Eric, and that was a kind offer, so he weighed his options, and his first two thoughts were, *Eric is good at this type of work* and *free food for a weekend.*

"You know what, Eric? I'll take you up on your offer. I'll spend the weekend with Mr. J."

"Great!" Eric exclaimed. "I'll call him and let him know that you'll head his way in the morning."

As they both headed to their bedrooms for the night, Bobby could only hope that what he agreed to would help him the same way it had helped his friend. Meanwhile, Eric could only hope that what he had arranged would help his friend the same way it had helped him.

CHAPTER 4

Bobby woke up earlier than usual the next morning. *What have I agreed to?* He started to pack two days' worth of his belongings. *I'm already behind on my project! I'm certain that I could make better use of this weekend catching up on my work rather than spending my time with some old guy I've never met.*

A knock on his bedroom's open door brought Bobby back into the present moment as Eric walked into the room, giving him a high-five.

"Bobby, I want you to know that I'm proud of you, bro. I imagine you think that it doesn't make sense to leave for the weekend and that it would make more sense to stay home and get your project done."

Bobby gave a slight nod, letting Eric know that he agreed. It was almost like Eric knew every thought that was racing through Bobby's head.

Eric continued. "That's logical reasoning, and I understand your point of view. Believe me, though, if you spend this weekend with Mr. J, open to the lessons that he's ready to teach, you will find the experience is completely worth it."

Bobby grabbed his coat and packed bag, and said, "Eric, even though I don't know what I've gotten myself into, I'll make the best of this weekend. See you later, bro." They gave each other a fist bump as Bobby walked out of the apartment.

Mr. J lived about an hour away. As Bobby drove toward Mr. J's house, his mind was racing with thoughts and questions coming from every direction. *Am I making another dumb decision? Shouldn't I be at home catching up on my work? Well, Eric seems to trust this guy. And when I think about it, Eric does seem like a completely different person than he was when we were in college. Maybe this Mr. J will help me with my life, which would be great because not too much has gone right. Why would he want to spend time with me, though? If he's as successful as Eric says he is, I certainly don't want to get in his way. I'm sure he has a million other things that he could be doing rather than spending time with me.*

Before Bobby knew it, he was arriving at the address that Eric had given him. Bobby was mind-blown as he drove up the elegant circular stone driveway to a huge brick house. *This is his house? You have got to be kidding me!* Parking his car in a spot facing the yard and house, Bobby remained seated and pressed the buttons to open all the car windows, letting the fresh country air surround him. He gazed at the well-kept grass and a yard more perfect than he had ever seen. The trimming of trees and bushes was excellent, and there wasn't a fallen leaf in sight. Bobby examined the outside of the magnificent house with steps up to the entrance of large double doors. He felt like the holiday season, which he thought he was missing, was lovingly displayed. There were single white candles aglow in each window. Through the large front bay window, he could see the twinkling lights of a fully-decorated Christmas tree. And the green wreath with a red ribbon on the door was the finishing touch. Bobby leaned his forehead on the steering wheel and mumbled to himself, "Please don't screw this up."

Lifting his head, Bobby saw the right front door to the house open, and a tall, well-dressed man with a big grin stepped out onto the porch and put his hands on his hips, looking over at Bobby's car. Then, he flung his arms open wide, like he was saying, "Welcome to my estate!"

"You must be Bobby!" Mr. J said with a chuckle as he walked toward the car. Bobby noticed many things at once: Mr. J walked with a limp favoring his right side, he was very well-groomed, his salt-and-pepper hair was in place, and his beard was neatly trimmed.

Bobby nervously extended his hand. "Yes, sir, I'm Bobby. You must be Mr. J."

Mr. J reached in through the open window and gave Bobby a big bear hug, totally surprising him. "Jack Owens, but my friends call me J." Reaching into the back seat, Mr. J added, "Let me grab your overnight bag! Come on in!"

As they walked toward the house, Bobby could sense Mr. J's genuine joy.

"I hope you're as ready for this weekend as I am!" Mr. J said with excitement.

This statement alone was perplexing to Bobby. *Why is this guy excited to spend the weekend with me? He doesn't even know me.*

Even though Bobby had just met Mr. J, the warm greeting increased Bobby's level of anticipation. He felt well-received into this man's home. Remembering Eric's words about his experience gave Bobby a feeling of peace. Though nervous, Bobby remembered what he had promised Eric and himself. *I'll make the best of my time here.*

CHAPTER 5

I n the comfortable guest room, Bobby noticed that he had everything he needed. On the desk, inside a brand-new State University coffee mug, was a note that read, *Welcome to our home. We hope to make this weekend one to remember.*

Smiling and feeling content, concern fading about his decision to be there, Bobby gazed around the room. *They sure do know how to treat their company! A guest room with a king-size bed? A bathroom to myself? A desk and television all for me? This setup is better than what I have at home.* Bobby was thankful to have a bathroom to himself since he and Eric shared one in their apartment.

Mr. J knocked on the door. "Come on, Bobby. Time for breakfast. My wife is ready for us!"

As Bobby followed Mr. J downstairs, his excitement grew as the aroma of the country breakfast filled the house. When he walked into the large kitchen, he admired the table setting ready to receive guests.

"Bobby, I want you to meet my wife, Ruby."

Ruby looked at Bobby and, with a smile that would light up any room, said, "Good morning, Bobby! Please make yourself at home. We have everything you need here. Don't hesitate to ask for anything."

Bobby responded warmly, "Nice to meet you, Mrs. Ruby."

Mr. J, grabbing his belly with both hands, said, "Okay, dear. What did you cook up for us today?"

"Well," Ruby responded, "we have buttermilk biscuits and pancakes, both made from scratch, of course. Bacon, eggs, grits, fried apples, orange juice, and hot tea! Bobby, I hope you enjoy."

Bobby stared at the table. She has all my favorites! How on earth did she know?

After saying the blessing, they all began to eat. After a few forkfuls of breakfast, a curious Bobby looked at Mr. J and said, "Mr. J, if you don't mind me asking, what do you do?"

Mr. J smiled as he responded, "Well, Bobby. I help people."

"You help people? In what way?" a perplexed Bobby asked.

"Well, nowadays, I help people with their finances—insurance, investments, financial planning, you know, those sorts of things. And I help many people. Before that, as I'm sure Eric told you, I played football at State University, which led to a brief career in the National Football League."

Bobby's eyes lit up with excitement, and he said, "You made it to the NFL? Wow! You must have made a lot of money!"

Mr. J chuckled and said, "Brief career. It ended with an injury. So, after that, I wasn't sure what to do, so I joined the Army. I served for eight years, and those experiences, coupled with my years of playing football, taught me teamwork, how to have a good work ethic, and the value of listening to authority."

Bobby gazed around the kitchen. He could tell that everything from the wooden floors, to the countertops, to each appliance, was of the highest quality. *He says that he had a brief career in the NFL. They must have paid him well during his career, or perhaps he received some sort of financial package due to his injury. I don't see how he's able to afford all of this by only helping people.* He looked at Mr. J and said, "Okay, please forgive me if I'm too forward. What did you do to be able to afford a house like this?"

This time, Mr. J leaned back and howled with laughter. "It's okay, Bobby. You can ask me any questions that come to mind." Still chuckling, he continued. "You see, I heard a quote a long time ago. It said something like, 'If you help enough people get what they want, you'll eventually get what you want.' So, although it didn't make complete sense to me, I figured I'd give it a shot. I began to learn about finances, and I found someone who was already successful, who could help me as I started my journey. I listened to every word he said. His words were like pure gold. And one thing I learned while talking with him was that he had the heart of a giver. I'll be honest. When I first started working with him, my mindset was, 'What can I get from people to help me succeed?' That soon transitioned to an open heart of, 'How can I genuinely serve people to be sure that they are well taken care of?' Before I knew it, my clients were hitting their goals, and I was well beyond the goals I had initially set for myself. It all started with taking my eyes off myself and learning to have the heart to help people."

Mr. J paused to enjoy the last mouthful of his breakfast and winked at his wife. Then he leaned in and said to Bobby, "Let me be clear. This weekend isn't about your finances. I want to learn about Bobby and see if I can be of any help."

Bobby stared at his host. *How can anyone help me? Why would a man this successful want to spend time with me? What do I have to offer?*

Smiling at him, Mr. J said, "So enough about me, Bobby. Tell me your story."

CHAPTER 6

Noticing the conversation's pause, Ruby spoke brightly. "Have y'all had enough to eat?"

Both men nodded, beaming at her.

"Thank you for such a wonderful meal!" Bobby exclaimed, standing up. "The last time I had a breakfast like that was when I was visiting my mom." He began to gather his dishes and utensils. "Where can I put my dishes?"

Ruby giggled, and with a motherly look, said, "Why, thank you, Bobby. And don't you worry about the dishes. You are the guest."

As Ruby began clearing the table, Bobby and Mr. J thanked her again, and Bobby followed Mr. J to a sitting room.

Bobby gazed around at many of Mr. J's accolades from playing football to his career in business. When Mr. J gestured to a brown leather chair, Bobby sat down, pondering Mr. J's request. *Share my story?* Bobby scanned memories and impressions of his life so far. *Which parts should I share? I haven't had much if any success at all compared to this guy. Well, what do I have to lose? I'm only here for a couple of days. I'll go for it.*

Bobby took a deep breath and started to share. "Well, Mr. J, I guess I'll give you a glimpse of my background. I'm the second of three of my parents' children. My parents divorced when I was nine years old. I took it pretty hard. I often wondered if I was the reason for their divorce."

Mr. J asked, "Why would you feel that you caused your parents' divorce?"

"Well," Bobby continued, "I never felt like my grades were high enough. My dad would always get on me and compare me to my older sister, who was an honor student. My mom would come to my defense, and before I knew it, they were arguing all over again. I figured that my grades must have been the reason."

Mr. J stopped Bobby and said, "Bobby, I want you to continue with your story, but please know that you are not the reason for your parents' divorce. I've counseled enough people to know that situations like your parents were in always have a deeper root. You just happened to witness some of the fruit of something that was already there. Anyway, go ahead and continue with your story."

Bobby paused briefly, pondering Mr. J's words. *For as long as I can remember, I have been sure that I was the reason for their divorce. And now, for the first time, I hear that I'm not the cause? He seems so confident in telling me that there must have been an influencing factor other than my grades. I want to believe him. I really want to believe him.* "Okay. Well, that experience had an impact on me. Somehow, I maintained a good relationship with my mom and my dad. But if I ever messed up in school or around the house, my mom would get frustrated with me. She would say things like, 'My goodness! You're just like your father!' And every time she would say that I wouldn't respond, and it hurt pretty badly. You know, she left my father. So, being like him couldn't be a good thing."

Mr. J, attentively listening, said, "I see. Go on."

Bobby continued. "I had to learn to find a good way to take out my frustration, so I started playing football. I ended up being a pretty good athlete. I played football in high school, which led to my college career at State University. Even though I never told them how I felt, I always looked to my coaches as fathers, mostly because my dad didn't seem to care too much about my athletic career. My coaches would get on me hard. They would always tell me that I wasn't living up to my potential. I remember one day, my position coach at State pulled our entire group together. We were the core strength of the team, and Coach always wanted us to get better. This particular huddle, he said, 'Guys, we have an opportunity to be the best defensive secondary in the entire conference. And Bobby, to be honest, you are the weakest link!'"

Bobby, needing a moment after reliving that situation, paused as he gathered his thoughts. "Mr. J, I can't tell you how that made me feel. I practiced hard after that with those words ringing in my mind. We ended up having a successful year, and I still wonder if I ever lived out my potential."

Mr. J, leaning back in his chair, seemed to be hanging on every word that came out of Bobby's mouth. "Okay, so what happened after college football?"

Bobby took a deep breath and sighed before continuing. "Let's see. I'm twenty-five now, so college wasn't too long ago. I ended up getting a job at a distribution company. I'm in a group of us training to be managers. I've had some success there, though it's pretty hard sometimes. While I am training to be a manager, I don't feel confident in what I'm doing. I often feel like I'm the weak link of the management training team. I'm always nervous about any project I'm given, and I've had trouble finishing strong. I'm waiting for the day when they find someone to replace me."

When Bobby finished sharing with Mr. J, they sat there for a brief moment in silence. It was a new feeling for Bobby to allow himself to be vulnerable, and he was hoping that Mr. J would not think any less of him.

Without a word, Mr. J got up and went into his office. When he returned a moment later carrying a brown leather bag, Mr. J pulled an apple out of it and asked Bobby, "What am I holding in my hand?"

Bobby looked at Mr. J, then looked at the apple in Mr. J's hand, then again, he looked directly into Mr. J's eyes. "An apple, of course. Is this some kind of trick question?" Bobby asked with a nervous laugh.

Mr. J chuckled. "Bobby, when you look at this apple, you only see a single apple. When I look at this apple, I see an orchard."

A perplexed Bobby looked at Mr. J and asked, "What do you mean you see an orchard?"

Bobby felt drawn to Mr. J without knowing why. Mr. J seemed to possess so much wisdom, yet he was so humble.

Sitting down again with both feet flat on the floor, Mr. J leaned forward and said, "Bobby, look here." He then took out his pocket knife and began to slice the apple. After slicing the apple, he pulled out each seed, placing them into his open palm. Nodding at the seed collection in his hand, he smiled at Bobby.

"How many seeds do you see?" asked Mr. J.

Bobby confidently responded. "Five."

Leaning back, Mr. J chuckled deeply and, looking at Bobby, said, "Let's take a look at what we have here. In every apple lies an orchard. Let's say there are five seeds in this apple. What we're going to do is take these five seeds, and plant them. It may be four to five years before we see an entire tree that produces apples. During this waiting period, we're going to do everything we can to nourish this seed to ensure that we're promoting a healthy apple tree that can produce six to ten bushels of fruit during the growing season. There are approximately one hundred apples in a bushel. So, let's say that each tree has ten bushels, you know, for easy math," Mr. J said with a smile. "Now, let's multiply ten times one hundred. Okay, let's see here, what do we get? Ah! One thousand apples! Wait a minute! Didn't we have five seeds?"

Bobby looked at Mr. J with amazement. He was still wondering about the point of this whole conversation about apples, mainly because it had immediately followed him feeling vulnerable in sharing his life story and difficulties. He simply said, "Yes, Mr. J. We had five seeds."

"Hot diggity dog!" Mr. J said with excitement. "When we multiply one thousand times five, what do we get? Five thousand apples, all from one apple! And remember, we're only talking about one harvest season."

Bobby had an anxious look in his eyes. *Okay. This demonstration is nice and all, but what is the point? How does this relate to all that I just shared with him?* "Mr. J, with all due respect, what is the point of this explanation? I see that I underestimated the value of an apple. What does it have to do with me?"

Crossing his legs and leaning back again, Mr. J spoke in a more serious tone. "Bobby, you have a mind, which is like soil. And in your mind, seeds have been planted throughout your life. Whether it be family members, friends, teachers, coaches, or teammates, people have said things about you. Any word said about you, whether positive or negative, is like a 'You are.' For example, when I went to boot camp, the drill sergeants called me every derogatory name you've ever heard. I realize now that it was my choice whether I would believe those insults or reject them. I struggled with this degrading treatment for quite some time. Remember, I was in the NFL. I felt like I was on top of the world. And now I'm being told everything I can't do? It was a rigorous mental battle, Bobby. And I was losing terribly. Then I remembered learning this concept from my college mentor. When you accept what someone says to you, those 'You are' words become 'I am' words, which are the most powerful words you can say to yourself. What you believe is what you become. I like to call those words spoken to you, 'spoken over you.' When you accept what someone speaks over you, you are planting a seed. Then, you have a choice: either nourish that seed to grow, or starve the seed so that it eventually dies. Remember, the apple trees that we planted were well-nourished, so they grew strong."

As Mr. J talked, Bobby grew more interested by the word.

Mr. J continued. "Now, let's look further. The words spoken over you have been positive or negative seeds, which have become your positive or negative thoughts. They've either given you life or have drained the life out of you. My question for you is, which seeds have you been nourishing?"

Bobby quietly considered words spoken over him through the years. How much life had he given to the negative words and insults from various people in his life? *Is it too late for me to turn this ship around?* Bobby felt earnestly hopeful, and at the same time, helpless. There was something about this conversation with Mr. J, though, that gave him the feeling that things could get better.

CHAPTER 7

M r. J and Bobby left Mrs. Ruby and headed for their first visit. The twenty-minute drive gave Bobby more time to think about his current situation. *It's strange enough to be spending the weekend with Mr. J, and now we are headed to someone else's home. Talk about nerve-racking. Well, this morning wasn't so bad. And the lesson about the seed made a lot of sense.*

Noticing Bobby was deep in thought, Mr. J said, "Bobby, I'm sure that Eric gave you some insight on what to expect. I also know that uncertainty can be unsettling. I promise that everything we do this weekend has a purpose, and I want you to get the most out of your experience."

Those few words helped settle Bobby, who smiled to show Mr. J that he received the message. Mr. J also smiled, acknowledging Bobby's improved comfort level, which was in good time as they turned into a neighborhood where there was enough space between the brick houses to give children room to play. They pulled up to a two-story brick home. As Mr. J parked his car, Bobby gazed at the property, which stirred up memories of his childhood. The wraparound porch with rocking chairs took him back to his summer visits at his grandmother's house. And the large, decorated windows reminded him of the quality time he spent with her decorating during the holiday season. Even though it was cold outside, inside, Bobby was beginning to feel warm.

Just as they were getting out of the car, a woman stepped out onto the porch.

"J! Come on in! I was wondering what took you so long!"

"Hey Rosa, how are you?! I have someone that I want you to meet. I was telling you about this young man. Here he is! Bobby, meet Rosa Rogers."

I wonder what he told her about me. He just met me this morning, so could he have possibly told her anything good about me? "Good afternoon Mrs. Rogers," Bobby said, extending his hand.

"Hi there, young fella. Why, aren't you a handsome young man!" Mrs. Rogers said to Bobby, taking his hand and winking at Mr. J.

While they stood together on the porch, they all watched a rabbit hopping across the front lawn.

"I tell ya," Mrs. Rogers said quietly, "where I'm from, that rabbit wouldn't have stood a chance!"

Mr. J and Mrs. Rogers laughed as they walked inside. Bobby chuckled uncomfortably, following them.

Mr. J and Mrs. Rogers were catching up on old times as they continued into the kitchen, leaving Bobby to look around. The house was more of a home than his basic bachelor pad of an apartment. Bobby could tell that family was important to Mrs. Rogers when he noticed many framed pictures lining the hallway walls. Bobby made his way to join them in the kitchen and, on the way, looked into the living area to the right where he could see freshly-pressed white table cloths hanging on a laundry rack. The sound of soft Christmas music filled the house. Bobby felt comforted by the warmth and love in the atmosphere created by Mrs. Rogers in her home. He was feeling eager to learn more about this mysterious woman. *I am not sure what to expect from my time here with Mrs. Rogers. I do know one thing for sure. She sure does know how to set a peaceful environment.* As he stepped through the kitchen entryway, Bobby paused, framed by poinsettias placed on either side of the door.

"Bobby, come on in here and have a seat. Make yourself at home. Here, let me take your coat."

"Thank you, Mrs. Rogers."

"Would y'all like a glass of lemonade?"

Mr. J chuckled and said, "Rosa, have I ever turned down a glass of your lemonade?" Turning to Bobby, Mr. J said with a huge grin, "You have no idea what you're in for, young man."

Bobby smiled and said, "Sure, I'll have a glass. Thank you."

"Well, let me get you all situated. I'll serve you your spaghetti, and we'll get this show on the road. Joe is out finishing up a job, and he'll be home soon to join us."

While Mrs. Rogers was preparing the plates, Bobby sat quietly and watched as Mr. J and Mrs. Rogers spoke easily with each other. They both appeared to have so much freedom. Bobby felt a yearning for something he had never fully experienced. *What is it like not to have a care in the world? They both seem to be so free. I would love to have that kind of peace.*

After Mrs. Rogers served everyone their food, she asked, "Now, do y'all need anything else? Once I sit down, you're on your own."

Laughing, Mr. J said, "I think we're good to go. Mind if I say a blessing?"

"Go ahead, J."

After he said a blessing over the food, they began to eat.

Mrs. Rogers said, "So Bobby, tell me a little about yourself."

Bobby, not sure what to say, said, "Well, I'm twenty-five years old. I'm the second of three siblings—I have an older brother and a younger sister. I was an athlete in high school and college." He paused, feeling self-conscious. "What else would you like to know?"

"Oh, that's enough right there. There's no reason to be nervous. For the next couple of hours, please look at me like family."

That welcome from Mrs. Rogers helped Bobby to feel more comfortable. He took a deep breath, finished his food, and asked for seconds.

"You're my kinda fella! I like company who enjoys my cooking. Go ahead and help yourself."

When they finished their food, Mr. J leaned back in his chair and said, "Now Rosa, the reason I brought Bobby over here is that I wanted him to hear some of your story. You have one of the most compelling stories I've ever heard, and I believe that Bobby and I can learn a lot from you today. So, if you're ready, we're all ears."

"Well, how far do you want me to go back?" she asked.

"You know, from the beginning."

Rosa took a deep breath and started. "Well, I grew up in the country. I'm from a large family. I was the oldest of eight children—I have three sisters and four brothers. My father was an auto mechanic, and my mother was a homemaker and a caregiver. Being the oldest, of course, I had to help Mama out with the cleaning and ironing and all that she did as a homemaker, especially when we were out of school. Now when they closed the school, I had even more time to help Mama with all the chores."

A confused Bobby asked, "Um, did you say 'closed the school'?"

"Why yes, J didn't tell you?"

Mr. J had such a massive grin on his face that Bobby was beginning to catch on. Even being with Mr. J for less than twenty-four hours, Bobby figured out that a story and a lesson were coming.

"No, he didn't tell me."

"Well, let me fill you in. I'm from a place called Prince Edward County. Back in 1959, a new law stated that the schools in Virginia were to integrate. From what I hear, while most schools integrated, there had been talk for quite some time that my home county would refuse. So instead of integrating, they shut our school system down for five years. I was only seven years old at the time, so I didn't fully understand what was taking place. All I knew was that I saw some white people marching and protesting because they didn't want their kids to go to school with us. I didn't understand because I lived such a sheltered life. I didn't understand white and black. We even worked on a farm with white families, and we all got along just fine. We knew that our skin was a different color, and our hair was a different texture, but that didn't make any difference to us. We learned that love and respect of others is the most important way to live, so we did. So, to see people protesting was pretty confusing, as I'm sure you can imagine."

Bobby sat there, stunned. *A school system actually shut down for five years because they did not want to integrate? That is such a significant hurdle, and beyond anything I have ever experienced. Yet, she's here in this lovely home.* He had never heard of these events, and to listen to a firsthand account was inspiring. Bobby realized that he was having lunch with a real-life hero. When he looked more closely at Mrs. Rogers, he saw slight wrinkles under her eyes. They didn't seem to be the wrinkles of tiredness, though. Instead, they seemed to represent strength and a strong sense of overcoming.

Mrs. Rogers continued. "Bobby, all my parents had to do, for us to go to school, was to move from one county to the other, but my Daddy said, 'No, you're staying right here to help your Mama.' So, for the entire five years, I was out of school."

"Wow, Mrs. Rogers. I can't even imagine what that was like."

"Yeah, well, around that time, being the oldest, when we would get together for family time, I would pick up any manual, encyclopedia, Bible, or whatever was around, and I would read to the family. You see, my Daddy only had a sixth-grade education, and my Mama couldn't read. All she could do was write her name. She only had a third-grade education."

"Really?" Bobby asked, having a hard time comprehending how someone could only make it to the third grade.

"That's right. Around this time, there was a census to see how many children were out of school. There was an organization that helped us out. To this day, I couldn't tell you where they came from; some white young adults would come and take us to a church, and we would have school in a basement. Bless their hearts. I guess they knew what was going on wasn't right, and they decided to do what they could to help us. They taught us numbers and colors, and for some reason, they sang a lot of songs. Even though it wasn't everything we needed, it did help a little."

Bobby interrupted. "You know, Mrs. Rogers, we didn't learn much in school about the white families that helped the black families. Was that common during your time?"

Mrs. Rogers replied, "Well, all white people weren't mean to us. There were nice ones, like the ones who were our neighbors and those who took us to the school. And there were mean ones, you know, the ones who protested so that we couldn't go to school."

"Okay, I see."

"Well, after those five years, they reopened the schools. I remember a chain being on those doors, so they had to break the chains for us to walk into the school. Once we got there, they placed us back into school according to our age. I was twelve years old, so they placed me in the seventh grade. I remember taking an aptitude test to assess my knowledge. I felt inadequate taking that test because there was so much that I didn't know. They mixed us into classes with kids who hadn't missed a beat. So, that sense of inadequacy continued to haunt me. From my time re-entering school through high school, it was a constant struggle. Imagine bringing your homework home and having no one to help you. Mind you, I had missed five years of school, so I was already behind. I didn't know how to study. And remember, my Daddy only had a sixth-grade education, so how could he help me? I constantly battled the feeling of never being smart enough all through high school."

"Mrs. Rogers, how did you do it? How did you make it? Those were extreme odds!"

"Well, Bobby, the odds were extreme. And a lot of my friends didn't make it. I saw so many friends get overwhelmed with school and decide to drop out. They felt that working their way through school was too much of a hurdle. However, I made up my mind to persevere through it all, no matter how tough it was. I made a lot of Cs and Ds and some Fs. I still persevered."

"Were your parents supportive?"

"Well, Mama was supportive. Daddy, that's a whole different story. I don't know if it was because of any jealousy he felt; it's just that he would punish me whenever I asked him for help. I guess that was his way of telling me not to ask him for help. On top of that, he knew Mama couldn't read, so he would tell me, 'You're gonna be just like your Mama' and 'You ain't worth two cents' and 'You ain't nothin.' I couldn't understand how or why my father would say these things to me. I guess he had a hard time handling his oldest daughter becoming a young woman."

While Mrs. Rogers talked, Bobby could remember a similar feeling from words spoken over him through the years. "Mrs. Rogers, I can relate there."

"Well, Bobby, somehow, I managed to graduate high school. A lot of my friends did not graduate. I would see them later on, and they would tell me that it was just too hard for them. Somehow, I made it."

"That must have been a great feeling, Mrs. Rogers."

"Yessir, it was. And come to think of it, I was the first person on my Daddy's side to graduate high school."

By this point, Bobby was in complete shock. *The first one to graduate high school?* Bobby was becoming increasingly amazed and intrigued by Mrs. Rogers' story. He could only anticipate what was next. Little did he know that what was to come would help him in his journey to freedom.

CHAPTER 8

Bobby's strongest desire was to continue sitting at the table with Mrs. Rogers and Mr. J and listening to Mrs. Rogers tell more of her incredible story. *Who is this Mr. J? And how did I end up having lunch with a modern-day hero such as Rosa Rogers?* So many questions continued to flood Bobby's mind.

"Now, Bobby, I want you to know something. Growing up in my shoes was not easy. My Daddy was always hard on me. To this day, I don't know why he treated me the way he did. I never had a single date because I feared what he would say or do. From time to time, boys would ask me out because, well, you know, I wasn't bad on the eyes."

Bobby repeated her words. "Not bad on the eyes?"

Mr. J and Mrs. Rogers laughed at the youngster.

Mr. J smiled at Bobby and said, "Bobby, that means that she was a looker, you know, the boys thought that she was attractive."

An informed Bobby smiled and said, "Ohhh. I see."

Mrs. Rogers continued. "Some would even come to the house, and my Daddy would embarrass me. I got to the point where I gave up and made up my mind that as long as I lived in his house, I would not date."

"Mrs. Rogers, that must have been hard. And you were a young adult by this time, right?"

"Right. Now let's see. Ah! Now I didn't tell you that my family worked in tobacco. When school was out during the summer months, we'd work out in the tobacco fields from sunup to sundown. And at the end of the week, the white people we worked for would give us five dollars."

Bobby could not believe what he just heard. "Five dollars?! That's it?!"

"Yessir. Five dollars. And sometimes, they wouldn't even give us that. I remember times when they paid my Mama with a chicken. They'd say something like, 'You have all them children in the house. I know you can use a chicken.' Now mind you, we worked all week long, and our only payment was a chicken."

"Mrs. Rogers, that just isn't right," Bobby quietly said while shaking his head.

"No, it wasn't. That's what happened, though. Now, let's see here. Around this time, I began to think about my future. I knew that I couldn't stay at home. And I tell ya, it was frustrating. Everybody around me looked like they had it together and seemed to know what they wanted to do. Me? I had no clue. There wasn't anybody in my family with any real profession, so I didn't have anyone to follow. All I knew was that I wanted to do better than my parents. I didn't necessarily look down on them because I knew that they did what they knew. I wanted better for myself. I tried typing and other things and concluded that they weren't suited for me. So, one day, I went back to my high school, and I saw a nurse. It was like a beam of light was shining on her. Her hair was in place, and her clothes, stockings, and shoes were snow-white. Everything about her was perfect. When I saw her, I made up my mind that I wanted to be a nurse."

"Wow. I can't say that I had a moment like that when choosing my job. That's like something out of a movie!"

"Yes, it was. So, after getting the proper paperwork from my high school, I ended up going to a vocational center. Now, here's the issue: I couldn't drive. I hadn't even been behind a steering wheel. I needed a ride because the vocational school was five miles from where I lived. So, I reluctantly asked my Daddy to take me to the school. He agreed. The rides to school were not peaceful. One day, he told me that I needed to find another way to school because he had other things to do. While he's saying this, all I could think was, 'I don't know anyone else with a car. How can I get to school?' On a separate occasion, Daddy said that I needed to give him some gas money. I told him that I didn't have any money because I had given it to Mama to help her with some things. Bobby, he slammed on the brakes and said, 'What?!' Then he told me to get out of his car."

Shocked, Bobby replied, "In the middle of the road?!"

"Yes, in the middle of the road, my Daddy put me out of his car. I was crying. Rather than turning around to go home, I kept walking toward the school, knowing that my Daddy would turn around to come get me. He never came back! So, I just kept walking, hugging my books in my arms. I ended up walking to a country store on the way to the school, crying the whole way there. Then, out of nowhere, a car pulls up to the service station. It ended up being one of the teachers from the school, who was also a local. He asked me, 'What are you doing standing out here by yourself?' When he asked me that, I burst into tears again and told him that my Daddy put me out of his car and that I had to find a way to school. Well, I guess he had sympathy for me. He said, 'I tell you what, I can take you to school today. And if you want, you can meet me here every day, and I'll take you to school.' I was relieved. I still had to walk about a mile to the service station. That was much better than having to walk all the way to school."

"I know you had to be relieved."

"Yes, relieved and thankful. Well, once I finished vocational school, it was time to find my placement. I knew that I didn't want to stay at home or close to home. With the positions filled in Farmville, all that was available was the Medical College of Virginia in Richmond, Virginia. Only thing is, even though I had no clue how I'd get there, I made up my mind that I would find a way.

"So, what did you do?"

"Well, as frightened as I was of his response, I ended up telling Daddy the situation and that I needed to be in

Richmond by a certain date. Now at this point, Mama was also in the room. She said, 'No, I don't want you going down there.' See, Bobby, you have to remember that to us, Richmond was a big city. We lived in the country, so going to a place like Richmond was foreign and scary. I set my mind to it. And you know what? To this day, I don't know what made my Daddy agree to take me down there. For my entire life, he was just so verbally abusive to me, so him helping me was nothing short of a miracle. Not only did he agree, but he also helped me find a place to live!"

"Really?"

"Yes, he did. He had a friend who was able to help me out. I guess at the end of the day, I was still his daughter, even though he didn't always treat me that way."

"Wow, Mrs. Rogers. That's a pretty sharp turn of events."

"Yes, it was, Bobby. Yes, it was."

CHAPTER 9

M rs. Rogers looked at the gentlemen sitting at her table and asked, "Would either of you like a re-fill of your lemonade? I would like to get up and walk a few steps before getting to the next part of my story."

"Sure, I'll have a refill, please," Bobby responded.

Mr. J chimed in, "Make that two, thanks."

While Mrs. Rogers carried their empty glasses to the counter, a smiling Mr. J looked at Bobby and said, "Well, what do you think?"

"I'm still processing right now. This story is a lot to absorb. From growing up in a community where your school is closed for five years to have a father be so verbally abusive, Mrs. Rogers sure has gone through a lot."

Walking back over to the table with full lemonade glasses, Mrs. Rogers said, "Well, now I'm going to tell you about the lingering effect of those circumstances on my journey to Richmond."

After sipping his lemonade, Bobby, smiling with anticipation, said, "I'm all ears."

"Well, I ended up renting a room in a lady's house in Richmond. When it was time to go to school, she gave me directions to the bus stop. Now mind you, I grew up in the country. I lived on a dirt road, so I didn't know anything about streets or blocks. And I didn't know anything about a bus. When she gave me directions on how to get to the bus stop, she could have been speaking Chinese because I didn't understand a word she said. Somehow, I figured it out. When I got to the bus stop, I was cold and scared. The bus stop was in front of a house. A lady stepped outside and asked me what I was doing. I told her that I was waiting for the bus. She said, 'Oh, you're early. That bus won't be here for a while. You want to step inside and wait?'"

Bobby's skeptical nature led him to ask, "A random lady invited you inside her house?"

"Yes, and even though I was fearful, I ended up stepping inside. You know, Richmond was a big city compared to my hometown. And you always heard stories of shootings and murders. This lady was nice, though. She asked me where I was going. I told her, and it turns out she worked in the same building! So, we ended up riding the bus together, and when we got to the Medical College of Virginia, or MCV like we call it, she showed me around and walked me to where I needed to be. I was so nervous and so thankful at the same time."

"It sounds like she must have been some angel sent just for you."

"That sounds about right. Now, Bobby, I ended up being at MCV for forty years."

Obviously more comfortable at this point, and continuously being thrilled by every word spoken by Mrs. Rogers, Bobby leaned forward and asked, "Forty years?!"

"You heard me right. I worked there for forty years. It wasn't always easy, though. I remember Mama telling me always to give my very best at whatever I did. So, when I got to MCV, I started as a nurse's aide. I was good at what I did. One of my supervisors took notice and recommended me to be a Licensed Practical Nurse. Me? An LPN? That was a big step. So, of course, with every promotion comes a test. It was almost like every time I studied for this test, I would hear Daddy's voice ringing in my ear saying, 'You ain't nothin'!' and 'You ain't worth two cents!' and 'You're gonna be just like your Mama.' Every time I would hear those words, it was like I had a ball and chain wrapped around my ankle, like a slave who could see my freedom and yet could not break free from the tormenting voices of my past. It was like those words were seeds, and they would show up when it was time for me to move forward. And if it wasn't my Daddy's voice, it was like every obstacle I ever had would flood my mind, and I would begin to feel sorry for myself. They became obstacles that I had to learn to overcome. You know, come to think of it, there always seemed to be some obstacle—the school closing, persevering through school to graduate, figuring out what job to do. And then there was getting a promotion. Each step was a significant obstacle in my life. Somehow, I overcame them all."

"Wow," Bobby said, being reminded of Mr. J's lesson about the power of seeds. Now he was sitting at the table with a real-life example of a seed that produced good fruit.

"Yeah. Well, don't get me wrong. Passing that test was hard. I felt like I had an anxiety attack every time I took that test. The people in the class just looked like they were better suited than I was. And of course, they hadn't been through what I had experienced to get there. It came to a point where I had to learn to stop feeling sorry for myself and realize that I was capable of passing the test. I took that test three times and finally passed on the third time."

"I know that must have been a great feeling."

"Yes, it was. Bobby, there were some women on my job who used to ask me why I cried so much. They began to spend time with me. When they said good things to me and about me, their words became louder than my Daddy's voice, and I felt liberated. It came to a point where I faced a decision: believe what my Daddy said about me or accept the good in me that these women saw. And you know what? I started to believe the women. I remember one particular registered nurse saying to me, 'So what if you don't pass the test the first time. Pick yourself up and try again.' As hard as that was for me, I believed her and held on to her words. I realized that all those bad things my Daddy said about me were a lie, and I would no longer entertain them. I stopped being a victim of my past, and I grasped a vision for my life. And that vision led to a forty-year career of working in a field of my passion."

Bobby contemplated Mrs. Rogers' transition from being a victim to having a vision.

Mrs. Rogers noticed that Bobby was in deep thought and paused for a moment before continuing. "You know, Bobby, after I retired, I began to reflect on my life, being out of school for five years to having a forty-year career as a nurse. I was so thankful to be a part of the institution and for the opportunity given to me that I went back to my department at MCV and told them my story. I could see that those obstacles had been opportunities for me to prove to myself that I was an overcomer. When I was there telling them my story, they mentioned something about me coming and speaking to the program as a retiree because they said my story would inspire somebody. Well, I'm still waiting on the call."

Bobby looked at Mrs. Rogers and said, "Mrs. Rogers, whether you get the call or not, please know that you've inspired me."

"Why, thank you, Bobby. That means a lot. It's only my story. Now, what will your story be?"

CHAPTER 10

Just as Mrs. Rogers finished sharing her story with Bobby and Mr. J, her husband walked in the door. "What's going on in here?! I don't smell no chicken, no biscuits, nothin'!"

"Oh, stop, Joe!" Mrs. Rogers said, laughing. "I told you we were having company!"

"What?! Oh, J! I didn't even see you there!"

Mr. J stood up while laughing and walked over to embrace his old friend. He knew that Joe Rogers always found a way to keep everyone in good cheer. "It's good to see you, Joe. How's the business coming along?"

"Well, the checks are still rolling in, and I'm still cashing them."

Everyone laughed, including Bobby, who could see that Joe Rogers was a friendly man with a good sense of humor.

"Well, young man, who are you, and why are you sitting in my chair?" Joe said while winking at Bobby.

"I'm Bobby. It's great to meet you, Mr. Rogers," Bobby said while smiling and extending his hand for a handshake.

"Great to meet you, Bobby. Do me a favor, though. Just call me Joe."

Mr. J turned to Bobby and said, "Now Bobby, Joe is here right on time. I want him to share some of his story with you, too. It's not the same as Rosa's, and I think you may be able to learn a thing or two from him."

"Sure thing, Mr. J." Bobby's eyes were bright as he turned to Rosa's husband and grinned. "I'd love to hear it, Joe."

"Well, young man, give me a couple of minutes to get situated, and I'll share my story with you. Rosa, did you save some of that spaghetti for me?"

"You know I did, Joe. Coming right up."

Joe looked at Bobby, smiled, and winked again. "Boy, one day you'll be lucky to have a woman like the one I've got."

Being attentive to the love that Joe and his wife had for each other and the natural interaction between them, Bobby replied, "I hope so, sir. I hope so."

"Well, being that I'm just getting here, could somebody fill me in on what's been going on?"

Mr. J said, "I can fill you in, Joe. So, Bobby is spending a couple of days with me. He was introduced to me by his friend, Eric."

"Oh, I remember Eric! That was a sharp young man. How is he doing?"

"He's doing great," Bobby said. "His business seems to be growing more and more each time we talk about it."

Joe burst with laughter, slapped his thigh, and said, "That's what I like to hear! I knew that boy would come around."

At this point, Bobby reflected for a moment on some of his conversations with Eric. *From the sound of things, it appears that Eric really has applied what he learned from his time with Mr. J.* Things were beginning to come full circle.

Mr. J continued. "Well, just before you walked in the door, Rosa shared her story with us. She shared from childhood to retirement."

"Well, did she tell you how I swept her off her feet?" Joe said while leaning back in his chair with a look of pride.

Mrs. Rogers smiled and said, "Look, Joe, your spaghetti is ready to eat. Say your blessing and carry on. And while you're saying your blessing, ask the good Lord to forgive you, because you know that when you saw me, you were stuttering like Porky Pig."

A stunned Joe said, "What?! Who?! Me?!"

Everyone burst out laughing as Joe began to eat his food.

Once Joe had finished eating, he pushed his plate away, winked at his wife, and leaned back in his chair once again. He appeared reflective while looking at Bobby sitting across the table from him. "Okay, Bobby," Joe began, "let's see. Where do I want to start? I was an only child. I grew up with my mother and father, and I spent a lot of time with my aunt because she had many children. She would let me come over to play with my cousins so that I wouldn't be alone. Life was good. We raised everything.

We had a farm that provided everything we needed from the food we grew in the garden to the cows in the fields."

"Joe, that must have been convenient to have all the food right where you were living."

"It was convenient, and it was also hard work. And you know, Bobby, growing up in that atmosphere was all I knew. I didn't know what I wanted to do once I graduated high school. I took a couple of carpentry and electrical classes, and I knew that I was pretty good. I was still unsure of what I wanted to do. I ended up joining the military at nineteen years old, where they trained me to become an electrician. I also learned a few other trades while I was in the military, such as being a mechanic. My time in the military ended early due to an honorable discharge."

"How long did you serve?" Bobby asked.

"I served for three years. And after I got out, I got a job working construction. You know, building houses. From there, I began to use my GI Bill to go to college. While I was in college, one of my relatives recommended that I begin working for the Department of Corrections, or DOC. That way, I'd be able to work, have some of my college fees taken care of, and have a little pocket change. Ain't nothin' wrong with a little pocket change, Bobby."

Bobby smiled and nodded.

"Well, apparently I was good at my job, Bobby. For some reason, I kept on getting promoted. After a while, I decided to put college on the back burner. I ended up working in the DOC for twenty-six years. I rose through the ranks and ended up becoming one of the highest-ranking officials in the state."

"And you did this without finishing college?"

"Yessir. Don't get me wrong. I still think about going back to college from time to time, and yes, I was indeed able to rise through the rankings without completing my degree."

"Well, Joe, I guess it pays to do a good job."

"You got that right, young man. And may I add that I kept a good attitude."

Bobby nodded in agreement.

"Well, while I was working for the DOC, I decided to start a business on the side. You see, I was a licensed contractor. I had a crew of men working for me, and I was able to work my job schedule in a way that allowed me to put good effort in my business. Now, Bobby, I always made sure that I did excellent work on my job. You know, they were paying me, so I wanted to be sure that I was giving them my best while I was there. Then, with my business, I had to stay focused to maximize my time."

"Joe, that's a lot! How did you work both a full-time job and have a successful business?"

"Well, let's go back to my childhood. I was ten or eleven years old when I remember walking to my cousin's house, and on my way there, I saw this nice home. The neighbors were outside, and they had a water hose. When I saw that, I knew that I wanted a house with running water and a water hose. Having a car was beyond my dream.

All I knew was that I wanted a house with running water and a water hose."

Young Bobby had a hard time comprehending what he was hearing. "Running water? Your house didn't have running water?"

"Bobby, the way I grew up, I thought you had to be rich to have running water. We didn't have electricity either. Even though we didn't have a luxurious life, we felt that we had all we needed."

"Joe, how did you go from having a house with no electricity and running water to having all that you have now? You seem to have made a pretty good life for yourself."

"Well, I had a clear vision. I knew what I wanted. To this day, I can perfectly describe that house that I saw as a youngster. My memory permanently holds the vision of that house. It's something about having a clear vision and then keeping your vision fresh. I also knew that if I wanted something, I had to make sacrifices."

Bobby reflected on his current state. Realizing that he had often allowed life's circumstances to cloud his mind from having a clear vision, he said, "I think I need to chew on that one, Joe."

"Bobby, let me give you a little more to chew. I remember telling a friend of mine that I wanted to make one million dollars. A couple years later, he asked me had I made my million. I looked at him, smiled, held up two fingers, and said, 'Two.'"

Mr. J and Joe got a kick out of watching Bobby's astonished look when he heard how much Joe had made within a couple of years' time frame.

"You see, Bobby, once again, I had a clear vision. I knew what I wanted, and I developed a plan to help me get there. I stayed focused, and even though it wasn't easy, I was able to reach my goals."

Bobby sat there, contemplating the simple steps that Joe laid out in front of him. *Have a clear vision, have a plan to get there, and stay focused, even when it's not easy. I think I can do this.*

"Joe and Rosa," Mr. J said, standing up, "I can't thank you enough for agreeing to help Bobby and me out today. Thank you for your time."

Bobby, clearly still pondering what Joe had just told him, also stood up. "Joe and Mrs. Rosa, thank you for your hospitality and sharing some of your life stories with me. You have given me a lot to think about."

After saying their goodbyes, Mr. J said, "Come on, Bobby, we have another stop to make."

CHAPTER 11

While Mr. J and Bobby were traveling along the road with Mr. J behind the wheel, the two men continued to dialogue about their lunch at the Rogers' house.

"So, what do you think, Bobby?"

"Wow. I'm still trying to comprehend everything I just heard. It's one thing to read stories like Mrs. Rogers' story in a book. Or even see it in a movie. Now, to hear her first-hand experience in person was amazing."

"And what about Mr. Rogers?"

"Well, I'm still trying to figure out how he went from having a dream of just wanting running water to having a successful career that has produced millions of dollars."

"It's amazing what a clear vision can do for you, Bobby. And once you achieve your goal, keeping a fresh vision is just as important."

As Mr. J was driving, Bobby was wondering what was next on the list. *Where are we headed now? I'm not sure that I can learn any more after our time with Mr. and Mrs. Rogers.* Within thirty seconds, Mr. J turned into a fire station and parked his car. *Why are we at a fire station? This surprise ought to be interesting.*

Mr. J was greeted by a firewoman, who stepped toward the car and smiled warmly at Mr. J as he got out of the vehicle.

Mr. J beckoned to Bobby. "Bobby, come on over here. I have someone who I want you to meet!"

Bobby walked over to join them and said, "Hi, nice to meet you. I'm Bobby."

"Great to meet you, Bobby. I'm Faith, Mr. J's niece."

Mr. J seemed to know his way around the place. "Okay, Faith, let's show Bobby around."

Faith went on to show Bobby the fire trucks. She explained the functions of each vehicle and described the purpose of each one.

Mr. J, obviously excited, blurted out, "Come on, Faith, let's get to the hoses."

Faith laughed, knowing that her uncle had a routine. She knew better than most because she'd sat through this lesson countless times. "Okay, Bobby. Here is the fire hose, and this is a water hose. They serve two purposes. The fire hose design handles a greater amount of pressure. It usually has several layers that are rubber alternating with fabric with the final outside layer being a thick layer of cloth. A garden hose usually handles only a minimum amount of pressure. The higher pressure of the fire hose produces more gallons per minute than any garden hose."

Mr. J butted in eagerly. "You see, Bobby, the fire hose is meant to extinguish fires. That's why it has thicker layers and higher pressure. The garden hose, on the other hand, is meant to water plants and wash cars. Completely different purposes."

Bobby looked at the hoses. *Okay. There isn't anything revolutionary about what Faith just said. I know by now that there must be a lesson somewhere. What am I missing?* "Mr. J, with all due respect, I think I could have figured this out. What are you getting at with the difference between these two hoses?"

Mr. J and Faith looked at each other and chuckled.

"You see, Bobby," Mr. J said, looking directly at Bobby, encouraging him to focus, "think of these hoses as tools for your thoughts, which, as you know, are the seeds that we talked about earlier. It's always up to you what you choose to do with your thoughts, positive or not so positive, shaped by your experiences. Let's look at Mrs. Rogers' story. Her father told her that she wasn't worth two cents. The bad seed of her father's words was like a spark to cause a destructive fire in her life. Now, it was up to her as her life went on to decide how she would handle that thought. Would she fan the flame produced by the spark by repeating it to herself and associating with people who helped to start the fire? Would she allow that thought to dominate and define her? Or would she choose to extinguish that thought by saying the opposite? Would she say to herself that her life has value and purpose? You see, you can always choose to extinguish a lie, which is like a destructive fire, by speaking the truth. The truth of the matter is that Mrs. Rogers' life, just like each of our lives, has value and purpose. She chose to eradicate the lie that she wasn't worth two cents and believe the truth that her life has purpose. That is why she was able to have a successful career. Once you extinguish any lies from your thoughts, you must learn to nourish the truth. And that is the purpose of the garden hose. Continue to speak it, and hang out with people who will build you up rather than tear you down."

Bobby stood there quietly with his thoughts as Mr. J and Faith smiled at each other and exchanged goodbyes. *A bad seed is like a spark that can cause a destructive fire in my life? Fan the flame produced by a spark or extinguish it? Nourish the truth? This concept is a lot to take in, and I'm not sure that I completely understand his point.*

"Thanks for helping me out again. You play a big role in helping a lot of people."

"Anytime, Uncle J. Anytime."

Mr. J and Bobby walked back to the car, climbed in, and prepared for their next destination.

As Mr. J started the car, Bobby said, "Mr. J, you said a lot back there. I'm trying to understand what you're saying. Can you elaborate a little more, please?"

Mr. J was quiet while he was turning out of the fire station's parking lot and onto the main road. Then he said, "Sure. Some people only focus on the negative things that have happened to them. You could look at that as being enslaved to their past. And Bobby, please don't get me wrong. I understand that some people have had to go through awful situations that I would not wish on my worst enemy. Whether it be the verbal abuse that you told me you received, or maybe it was a past failure in the classroom or athletics. The separator is an individual's response to adverse situations."

Mr. J paused to allow Bobby a moment of reflection. Then he continued. "Let's look at Mrs. Rogers' situation. When she was seven years old, she was not allowed to attend school in her community because of her skin color. She was then out of school for five years. At the age of twelve, she was put back in school and told to survive. While all of this turmoil was happening, she had a father who told her time and time again that 'she ain't nothin'' and that her life wouldn't amount to anything. Of course, she had to deal with the situations and the words spoken over her, so let's review her outcome. She battled through high school, went on to college, and had a successful career as a nurse. You don't make it that far by only focusing on your trials. Just like the apple seed we talked about earlier, she had a choice of which seed she would water. She watered the liberating seed which happened to be the voice telling her that 'she could do it.' She used the hurt and circumstances to help drive her to a successful career."

Bobby sat there quietly, considering each word that came from Mr. J's mouth. He recalled sitting at Mrs. Rogers' table and the feeling of being able to relate to her story. *How many times have I given life to my mother's words? How many times has she told me that I'll be just like my father? How often have I allowed those words to shape my performance in school, on the field, or at work?*

When Mr. J stopped the car at a stoplight, he turned to Bobby who was staring at Mr. J, about to speak. Before he could say a word, though, Mr. J looked deeply into Bobby's eyes and said, "Everyone has trials, Bobby. It's how you respond to those trials that is a choice that you make. Remember, you have to know when to extinguish and when to nourish."

CHAPTER 12

M r. J and Bobby walked up to the door of the coffee shop. As they stepped through the entrance, Mr. J spotted his longtime friend, Benny. They greeted each other with a hug.

Mr. J turned to Bobby and said, "Bobby, meet my good friend, Benny."

"Benny?" Bobby asked softly while still digesting Mr. J's lesson from the fire station.

"Yes, Benny. His last name is Bennett, and back in our service days, he was known as Benny."

"It's nice to meet you, Mr. Bennett," Bobby said while extending his handshake.

"Glad to meet you too, young fella," Benny said with a smile. "Come on and have a seat. Want something to drink? This place has the best coffee in town!"

Bobby wasn't sure how to answer. He wasn't much of a coffee drinker, and at the same time, he wanted to be respectful of Mr. Bennett's offer. After taking a second to think, he blurted out, "Coffee with plenty of cream and sugar!" He figured that the cream and sugar would drown out the taste of the coffee.

Mr. J, chuckling at Bobby's response, told Benny to order his usual. As they continued exchanging pleasantries, Mr. J explained to Benny that Bobby was a young man who was spending a couple of days with him. "Benny, I'm introducing Bobby to a few people around town to hear some of their stories. You know how I love a good story—I'm sure you remember from our days in the service."

Benny laughed and said, "I love telling a good story about as much as you love hearing 'em!"

They both laughed while Bobby sat there smiling, unsure of where he fit in at that point. Thankfully, they were interrupted by the waitress, who set their coffees on the table.

"Benny, tell Bobby some of your story. You know, tell him some of your family's story—the one we talked about not too long ago."

Benny sipped his coffee and leaned back in his chair. "Let's see, where do I start? I remember taking my family out to California years ago for a vacation to visit my dad. He was a sharp man, and he read a lot. I remember talking with him about our family's lineage. You see, my mother had left him when my brother and I were children because of poor decisions that he continued to make. She did not want those decisions to affect us. What I didn't know when I was a child," Benny said as he sat up straight in his chair, "was that my grandfather had also left my grandmother. And that's not the end of it. My great-grandfather had left my great-grandmother! Bobby, that's three generations of men in my family whose marriages ended in divorce."

Bobby noticed that the more Benny talked, the more he leaned in, and the more demonstrative he was with his hands. Bobby was reflecting on what Mr. J had explained to him about the power of a seed. He was trying to make sense of how that lesson worked within Benny's story. "So, what about you, Mr. Bennett, I mean, Benny? If you don't mind me asking, what about your family?"

"Well, I'm glad you asked. You see, when my oldest daughter was a toddler, I was very much on that same path. I was fed up with my wife and with my marriage as a whole. I moved out, and I also bought another house! Yessir. In my mind, the marriage was over. My wife and I were separated for a year and a half and on our way to being divorced. The Bennett family legacy was well on its way to staying strong! And then one day, the strangest thing happened: I got a vision."

Bobby, captivated and wanting to understand Benny, repeated, "A vision?"

"That's right, son. A vision; it hit me one day. I was on the same path as the three generations before me. I remembered the feeling of not having my father home with me. I did not want my children to have the same experience. So, as humbling as it was, I went home to my wife. We were two kids ourselves who did not have much of a sense of direction. We didn't know what we were doing. All we knew was that we wanted to make it work."

"Well, how did you do it?"

"You wouldn't believe it if I told you," Benny said with a smile. "So, I will tell you what happened anyway! Right around that time, I met another military man named Doug. This guy had the brightest smile and was one of the most genuine guys that I'd ever met! For some reason, he took a particular interest in me. Every time I was around him, I noticed that he had a sincere sense of joy that I had never experienced. He and his wife got along great and had already been married for twenty years. There was something inside of me that knew that my life would be better with this guy in it. Boy, I tell ya. There were times when Mrs. Bennett and I would be arguing, and out of nowhere, the phone would ring. And guess who it was?!"

"Who?!"

"Doug! I don't know how he did it! He always called at the right time. After a while, I began to spend more time with him voluntarily. I saw that he had a thriving marriage, and I desired the same thing for my marriage. I would ask questions, and he would answer. Thinking back, even though some of my questions were pretty silly, he never made me feel that way. He always took his time and did whatever he could to help me. He helped my vision become a reality."

"That's amazing. Wow. Benny, you wouldn't know that I come from a similar background. My parents are also divorced. I've often acted like it doesn't bother me, but it does. I'm not married yet, and I'm not sure that I want to be. You seem to have learned a few things from Doug. What else helped you to be where you are today?"

"Well, I will never forget the day I was driving home and was feeling frustrated with my wife. I kept asking myself, 'why are we so opposite?' Our opposing characteristics seemed to be driving us further and further apart. Then, out of nowhere, this thought hit me: A socket and a plug. They serve different purposes. Two plugs, nothing happens. Two sockets, nothing happens. When I realized that the meaning of the pair is to complement, I saw that her strengths help me, and my strengths help her. I learned that rather than despising our differences, it would be better to be thankful for how they enabled us to be a better team. That mindset helped change the outlook on my marriage."

"Wow. I've never thought of it that way."

"Yeah, Bobby, neither had I. You see, I don't claim to know everything. When I tell you my story, I can look at three things that helped me: having a vision for a successful marriage, having a mentor like Doug, and realizing how Mrs. Bennett and I complement each other. That vision inspired my willingness to be accountable and to learn and apply lessons along the way. And you want to hear the kicker?"

"What's that?"

"Well, my wife and I have been married for forty-five years, our oldest daughter is coming up on her twentieth wedding anniversary, our son has been married for ten years, and our youngest daughter is in her fifth year of marriage. You see, my desire, and ultimately, my decisions helped change the course of my family's history. My children don't have to look any further than their parents for a successful marriage. Once again, while I don't claim to know everything, I am thankful that I listened to my mentor, and now my children know that they can listen to me."

Mr. J chuckled and said, "Now, how about that?! Bobby, remember the seeds and the fruit they produce? And remember our trip to the fire station?"

"Yes, Mr. J. Things are starting to make sense."

As Bobby and Mr. J said goodbye to Benny, Bobby continued to muse about the story that he had just heard. *If Benny could reverse the trend in his family, what can I do for my own?*

Bobby and Mr. J talked in the car on their way back to Mr. J's house. Their visits for the day were complete, and Bobby was beginning to feel a sense of hope.

CHAPTER 13

Bobby woke up the next morning, feeling more rested than he had in a long time. *I guess a comfortable bed can make a world of difference.* Bobby stretched and hopped out of bed, ready for the day. After getting dressed, he went downstairs to the kitchen to see what Mrs. Owens had cooked up for breakfast. It was a little lighter than the day before. Before she went out on an errand, Mrs. Owens laid out choices of fruit, berries, granola, yogurt, and juice for the men to enjoy.

Mr. J smiled and said, "Well, good morning, sir! How did you sleep?"

Bobby responded, "Best rest I've had in quite some time."

"Well, I'm glad to hear it, Bobby."

While enjoying breakfast together, they continued to talk about each story and lesson from the day before.

"You know, Mr. J, those were some pretty amazing lessons. Since last night, I have thought about my life, and I've been wondering, how can I apply the lessons from each story?"

Mr. J could sense the spark of hope in Bobby, so after they finished breakfast and cleared the table, Mr. J said, "We'll find the answer to your question in the pantry." Together, they walked over to an open box on the counter. "Bobby, take a look at this box. What do you see?"

Bobby examined the box full of dented cans. *Why would someone keep a box of dented cans? Especially someone as wealthy Mr. J?* Having worked in a grocery store as a teenager, Bobby remembered the term "damaged goods." So, after giving it some more thought, and by this time knowing that Mr. J always seemed to have a lesson, Bobby confidently replied, "Damaged goods."

With a giggle, Mr. J responded, "Bingo! Right on the money!"

Mr. J reached into the pantry cupboard above the counter and pulled out canned foods that were in perfect condition. "Now, tell me what you see."

Bobby scanned the collection of cans while trying to figure out the point of this exercise and said, "Canned goods."

"Right again!" Mr. J said, grinning. Setting a dented can of soup beside a soup can in perfect condition, he said, "Now, tell me the difference between these two cans of soup."

Bobby began to get anxious. This question was silly. It was obvious that there was nothing wrong with one can, and the other had a dent. *The answer is right in front of me, and I know by now that I should be looking beyond what's obvious. Where is he going with this?*

"There is a dent in one can and not in the other," a curious Bobby said.

"Okay, now here is the million-dollar question," Mr. J said while he walked back into the kitchen, opened a drawer, and pulled out a can opener that Bobby noticed was in pristine condition. "What is on the inside of the two cans?"

While Mr. J awaited Bobby's answer, he pulled out two soup bowls and brought them, along with the can opener, into the pantry and placed them on the counter beside the two cans in front of Bobby's anxious gaze. Mr. J opened the cans and said, "Now Bobby, take a look at what we have here. We're looking at two soup cans; one's dented, and one's not. If you were to go to a salvage grocery store, you would pay less for the damaged can than you would pay at a general grocery store for the can in perfect condition. Why? Well, the answer is simple. Most people are not willing to buy damaged goods. To the customer and to the retailer, the damaged goods have lost their value. Even if what's inside is not damaged, the tendency is to stay away and to look for something that is in perfect condition."

Bobby looked at Mr. J without saying a word.

Pouring a can of soup into each bowl, Mr. J said, "Now look at what's being poured into the bowls. Two cans of soup. Same content. Same expiration date on the cans. Same amount of soup. The only difference is the container. To the average person, the dented can has lost its value. It's up to you to decide if you want to look at the outward appearance, or if you are willing to open the can and see what's inside."

Bobby stared down at the two bowls of soup. *Open the can and see what's inside. I think he's telling me to look beyond face value.* In a matter of minutes, his mind went from thinking that Mr. J was trying to convince him about the advantages of shopping at the closest salvage grocery store to realizing there was a more profound message to understand within this action.

"Okay, Mr. J. I think I get what you're saying. Do you mean that it is what's inside that counts?"

Mr. J chuckled and said, "Young man, that's only half of it. Yes, what is inside a container indeed is what's important. Now, let's take a further look. Can you imagine that people are like cans? One person may feel damaged by the poor decisions they have made. Another person may feel damaged by terrible things that they have experienced that were beyond their control. People can have a scar and feel damaged from words spoken or actions done to them, or a physical ailment. It is up to that person whether or not to accept the designation of 'damaged goods' as a final destiny. You see, it is your choice how you see yourself. Do you choose to see yourself as damaged goods, or do you choose to see the value that your life still holds? Yes! Damaged by your past or not, your life has value! So, my question for you, my young friend, is, do you believe it? Do you believe that your life has value?"

As Mr. J finished speaking, Bobby stood there in deep thought. *How much and what kind of meaning have I given to my past? Have I devalued the man that I have become based on bad things that happened in my life? Is this hole too deep for me to recover?* One thing for certain: Bobby felt his perspective shift when Mr. J told him that his life has value, changing the way that Bobby thought of himself.

CHAPTER 14

Following the conversation about damaged goods, Mr. J told Bobby that it was okay to relax in the sitting room for a while. He let Bobby know that they would soon be heading into town because there was another friend for Bobby to meet. Time flew by as Bobby continued to ponder the concept of damaged goods. *Despite the negative experiences from my past that have hurt me, that damage is to the container. My life is the content, and it still holds value.*

Before he knew it, Mr. J appeared at the door of the sitting room and said, "It's time to head into town!" So, they got into Mr. J's car and headed toward the first destination of the day. As they drove along, Bobby wondered where they were going. Within fifteen minutes, Mr. J parked the car in front of a downtown office building. As they got out of the vehicle, Bobby noticed the vinyl on the glass door that read *Appeals Division Office Building*.

"Come on, Bobby!" Mr. J said with excitement. "My friend Willie is waiting for us."

As Mr. J and Bobby entered the building, the concierge at the front desk greeted them. "Are you here for Mr. Noland?"

"Yes," Mr. J answered with a smile that would brighten anyone's day.

The concierge smiled in return. "Great. He's been waiting for you. I will let him know that you're here. Please feel free to have a seat while he makes his way down."

After thanking the front desk worker, Mr. J and Bobby sat down in the leather chairs nearby. Bobby gazed around the office with anticipation about their meeting with this lawyer. Minutes later, he heard a "ding!" He watched as the elevator door opened, and a middle-aged man dressed in a suit carefully made his way toward the sitting area.

Mr. J stood up and stepped forward, meeting him halfway, exclaiming, "Willie Noland!"

While the men were exchanging greetings, Bobby walked over to introduce himself. "Hi, Mr. Noland, my name is Bobby."

Willie laughed and extended his hand. "Great to meet you, Bobby. Please call me Willie. Come on up. I have lunch waiting for us in my conference room."

When they arrived at the conference room, Willie gestured at the table that held a spread of cold cut subs and cans of soda. "I was sure to order a variety of options for us. Please, eat all you want."

Eat all you want? Bobby smiled. *That's music to my ears!*

They settled themselves in chairs at the table, and while they were eating, Mr. J and Willie chatted about old times. Through careful observation, Bobby realized that Willie could not see very well, which explained his mindful walking earlier.

As Bobby reached for another sub, Mr. J said, "Well Bobby, I think you know what's coming next. I brought you here because, like us, Willie also graduated from State University. I had the opportunity to serve as his mentor for a semester, and let me tell you, I probably learned more from him during our time together than he learned from me!"

Willie laughed and said, "Come on, Mr. J. You're making me look better than I am." Turning toward Bobby, Willie began sharing his story. "First, Bobby, I want to tell you what an honor it is for me to meet you. I know that if Mr. J has decided to spend time with you that you must be special."

Bobby smiled and said, "Well, I don't know about all that. I'm just thankful that Mr. J has welcomed me and introduced me to people like you. So, Willie, I'm anxious to know your story."

Willie leaned back in his leather chair and began. "I was eleven years old, and I was very active in my neighborhood sports league. You name the sport, and I played it, baseball, basketball, football, track and field; shoot, I even tried soccer," Willie said while chuckling. "One day, my teammates and I were waiting for our baseball coach to show up at practice, and we figured that we would warm up without him. Our normal catcher wasn't there, and since I never had an opportunity to play the position in our games, I volunteered to be the catcher while we waited for coach. Without the coach there, we didn't have any of the catcher's equipment. I was taking a risk that any of us would do at eleven. One of our normal pitchers decided that he would help us get warmed up. When the first batter came up, another teammate said, 'Hey, look! Brandon has a BB gun!' Like everyone else, I looked over at Brandon, who was to my right. Here was the problem: the pitcher didn't see me looking at Brandon, so he threw the ball. When the batter swung, the ball grazed the tip of his bat and kept on moving. As I turned back from looking at Brandon and his BB gun, the ball hit me right in my eye."

Bobby remembered playing baseball when he was younger. "My goodness! Getting hit was always my biggest fear!"

"Well," Willie responded, "getting hit turned out to be my reality. To help you understand my medical background, I was born with cataracts, which had run through my family on my mother's side."

"Cataracts?" Bobby asked.

"Yeah, cataracts. Having cataracts is like a clouding of the lens of your eye that is normally clear. For people who have cataracts, seeing through cloudy lenses is a bit like looking through a frosty or fogged-up window."

"Oh, okay," an informed Bobby responded.

Willie continued. "So, as you can see, Bobby, getting hit in the eye with that baseball was the last thing that I needed. I had already had four eye surgeries, and this was just another setback. I already could barely see with my left eye because of the surgeries, and it just so happened that I got hit in my right eye. My vision didn't end right away. I even went to school the next day, like everything was fine. Over time, my eye began to bother me. My parents took me to the eye doctor, and he gave me some basic instructions that would help me. After a couple of days, while it didn't hurt anymore, my vision was starting to blur, which led to my becoming completely blind in my right eye. Now, remember that I could already barely see out of my left eye. So, by then, I couldn't see jack! And what was tough, Bobby, was that I lived right across the street from the athletic fields. Hearing my friends playing ball was hard because naturally, everything within me wanted to go out there and play with them. I knew that my limited eyesight wouldn't allow me to." Willie's recollection transported back to that time of hearing his friends outside; he gazed off toward the far wall. "To go from being so active to not being able to see my hand in front of my face was hard."

Willie paused and looked in Bobby's direction. "You know, Bobby, I was pretty stubborn, too. I didn't want to accept the fact that I was unable to see. Around that time, my friends and I had to walk about a mile to school. Before my vision hit its low point, I remember having to walk to school one day, thinking that I could manage it. The conditions weren't the best; it was foggy, and there were no sidewalks. I typically rely on my hearing quite a bit, and I was able to see just enough to be able to make out the path ahead of me. Well, this particular morning, my routine was to cross over to the left side of the street to face the oncoming traffic. As soon as I stepped onto the street, I saw the bumper of a brown Cadillac right up on me. That was the last thing I remembered until I woke up on the opposite side of the street with my head on the curb. I could feel a bad cut on my face and I could taste blood. I remember people crowding around me saying, 'Don't get up! Don't move!'"

Bobby was startled. The lawyer's story was drawing him in with every word spoken.

Willie continued. "Here I was, struggling with my eyesight and not wanting to acknowledge the depth of my struggle. I was hit by a car due to my lack of acknowledgment. The impact was so dramatic that a brand-new shoe had flown off one of my feet. When I woke up, I don't know if I was more upset about being hit by that car, or losing one of my shoes!"

They all laughed.

"Well, the amazing thing is that I walked away from that incident with no broken bones," Willie said, shaking his head. "All I had was minor cuts and bruises."

Mr. J looked at Bobby and said, "Isn't that something?!"

Bobby nodded in agreement; eyes wide.

"School let out about a month later," Willie said, "and I remember all of my friends walking home. At this time, I was still dealing with denial. In my condition, it took a situation for me to see what I couldn't see. I remember getting impatient. You know, that last-day-of-school feeling.

I was ready to go home like everyone else. I had to wait on my dad, though, who took longer than I was willing to wait. Once again, being stubborn, I decided to walk home. I remember getting to an intersection and seeing my dad. I yelled out to him, 'Dad!' I don't know if he heard me. I decided to run across the street to try to catch him. Well, that was a mistake. There was a car coming, and I misjudged the speed of the vehicle. It was probably traveling thirty-five miles per hour. I hesitated. I started— then stopped. Then it happened again—boom! Next thing I recall was my face hitting the windshield. Everything seemed to pause. I don't remember much. Maybe I lost consciousness. Somehow, my dad found me and made his way over to the scene of the incident. You know, my dad is a preacher. The way he tells the story, everyone thought I was dead at that moment. He prayed for me. Bobby, all I know is that I'm still here and able to tell you this story."

Bobby was stunned, speechless. *He was born with impaired eyesight, hit by a baseball in his better eye as a child, and then hit by a car—twice! One of those scenarios would be tough to deal with on its own, and he dealt with them all.* Willie's story seemed to get worse and worse by the minute. And yet, somehow, they were sitting in a conference room in an office with this remarkable man's name on the door.

CHAPTER 15

S o many thoughts continued to race through Bobby's mind. *How could a guy go from being legally blind to becoming an attorney?* Mr. J's lesson about damaged goods was brought to life now that Bobby was in Willie's presence and hearing some of his story.

Willie sensed that Bobby had many questions. "You know, Bobby, those two car incidents were directly related to my eyesight. Both incidents happened within sixty days of me getting hit in the eye with the baseball. Over that time, my eyesight got worse and worse. Looking back, I'm glad that it happened when it did because it gave my parents and me time to take a look at my situation over the summer and consider the best options for my schooling. I had to attend sessions with a mobility specialist, and I had to learn how to walk with a cane. I was losing confidence day by day. I was afraid to cross a busy intersection or any street for that matter. The mobility sessions taught me how to gain confidence in what I could see and how to rely on my hearing."

Mr. J interrupted at that point and said, "You know, sometimes you have to learn how to focus on what you have rather than on what you don't."

Willie nodded in agreement, and said, "Absolutely, Mr. J, you are right. And you know, that's what I did. I learned to put more of an emphasis on my hearing. I also learned to read and type with braille, and had to transition to using audiobooks. It wasn't easy. I had limited vision, and it was tough because of my age. I was a teenager, and we all know that teenagers can be brutal. I seemed to be the focus of every joke. I had to learn to deal with it. To this day, I'm thankful for my family. They were my foundation and my biggest support."

At a brief pause, Bobby reflected on some of the setbacks that he faced in his life. *I admire Willie's reliance on his family for support during his rough trial with his eyesight. How often have I tried to handle the tough situations all on my own? I may not have had the level of family support he had, but I did have coaches and teachers who showed me that they had my back. And now, I have my roommate, Eric.*

The sound of the intriguing storyteller's voice drew Bobby's attention back to the room when Willie continued speaking. "I remember that over time, the vision in my left eye began to improve. I didn't know what was happening, so I just told my parents. They took me to the doctor's office, and the doctor took a look at my eye. After the exam, he called in other doctors to look at my eye for a second opinion. Then he said, 'I don't have an explanation for this. Your retina seems to have reattached to the eyeball. I can't tell you how much your vision will improve, but it will get better. It seems like some kind of miracle!' Bobby, all I know is that I was thankful. Although I was still blind, I was able to recover some of my eyesight."

Reaching for a can of soda, Willie paused to open it and take a sip before continuing.

Bobby looked at Mr. J, who was looking at him with raised eyebrows, nodding.

"Right around this time," Willie said with wonder in his voice, "a high school for the gifted and talented accepted me as a student! I also had to switch tutors because my parents thought that I had become too dependent upon my tutor. I was frustrated. I didn't get off to a good start at the school. My grades were so bad that the administration was on the verge of disqualifying me from the school. They recommended that my parents place me in a school where I could learn a trade. I remember my dad looking at me and saying, 'Son, we haven't heard from you. Tell us, what do you want to do?' I looked at him and said, 'Give me another year. If I don't succeed, I will decide to leave.'

"You know, Bobby, I just wanted to give myself a chance. I had a choice to make: would I be enslaved to my handicap? Or would I learn to master it? Would I choose to be victim? Or would I search down deep inside to find the victory? Well, I decided to master my situation. I resolved to triumph over my circumstances—and I'm glad that I did. The next year, I won the 'Most Improved Student Award.' I also took an extra course and attended summer school. I was capable of more than what I had shown, and

I looked at this award as an opportunity to prove it. I had trouble with my eyesight, but there was nothing wrong with my brain. My biggest obstacle was myself. Once I got over myself and realized that my lack of focus in school was only hurting me, that's where the improvement began. And that improvement led to a full academic scholarship to State University. You see, I allowed my vision of going to college to override my lack of eyesight, and that vision became my focus. And I heard a lot of people telling me what I could and couldn't do. I chose to believe the voices that spoke life into me, namely, those of my parents.

"Once I got to college, my biggest obstacle was overcoming the fact that I was a vision-impaired student. I also dealt with people forming opinions of me before getting to know me. However, I turned it around and found a way to use it to my advantage. I would get preferential seating and always chose to sit in the front of the class on the far-right side, knowing that my left eye was my stronger eye. I would get to know the professors and allow them to know me. And I always made sure to get an A on the first test. I started as a math major. The only problem was that when you get to the higher levels of math, you have to see what the professor is writing on the board. The defining moment was during a particular calculus class. The professor wrote one math problem on three different boards going around the room. At that point, I knew that I had a decision on my hands. I ended up changing my major to Legal Studies and Public Administration."

Mr. J interrupted again and said, "Bobby, sometimes you have to learn how to evaluate your situation and make decisions that best suit your strengths. Some will look at Willie as one who quit his math studies. In reality, he made the best decision for his current circumstance. He was smart enough to realize that he could find another way to set himself up for success, and that's what he did."

Willie agreed. "That's exactly right. I simply chose a different path to be successful. It wasn't easy, but I did it. That decision led to being accepted into a top-five law school and receiving a scholarship for my tuition. Once I got there, I realized that I didn't get the same treatment as I did in undergrad. My acceptance into the school showed my classmates that I had earned my way there. I ended up being successful in law school, and I graduated with honors.

"Looking back, I'm thankful for the decision that I made of not allowing my eyesight to be too big of an obstacle. I'm glad that I turned what seemed like an obstacle into an opportunity, bringing me to where I am today. In the positions I've held throughout my career, I've managed as many as fifty people. And I'm currently still an attorney as we sit here today."

Bobby stared at Willie with awe. The story he had shared was a living demonstration of every nugget of Mr. J's teachings. *It's like he heard each lesson that Mr. J has taught me so far this weekend—the power of a seed and knowing when to water a seed versus when to extinguish a damaging thought. Willie has proven not to be damaged goods, and he's also found ways to turn every obstacle into an opportunity. If he can do it, perhaps I can do it too.*

As Mr. J stood up, he thanked Willie for his time and lunch the three shared.

Bobby also stood up and reached for Willie's hand. "Thank you for sharing your story, Willie, you've given me a lot to think about!"

"My pleasure, young man. I wish you miracles on your journey, too!" Willie shook Bobby's hand and smiled.

Mr. J and Bobby were silent as they took the elevator down to the lobby. Bobby recalled the conversation he had with Eric before meeting Mr. J, which seemed like a month ago with everything that had happened, and the weekend was not over yet.

The concierge smiled and nodded as they walked by, making their way out the door into the fresh December air. Mr. J grabbed Bobby by the shoulder and said, "Come on, it's time to head back to my house, get some rest, and then have a special dinner tonight with my bride."

CHAPTER 16

When Bobby and Mr. J arrived back to Mr. J's estate, Mr. J told Bobby, "You can go ahead and get some rest. I know that this has been a full two days, and I want to be sure that you're well-rested for dinner. My wife, Ruby, is preparing one of her famous dishes."

Bobby, remembering that he had to work in the morning, figured that he'd take advantage of a break. He replied, "Sure. What time should I be down for dinner?"

"Six o'clock."

A very familiar aroma was filling the house as he walked along the hall toward his guest room. Although excited and anxious for another meal with Mr. J and Mrs. Ruby, Bobby decided that getting some rest would serve him well.

Right at six o'clock, a refreshed Bobby came downstairs to a beautiful table set and ready to receive his company. The fine china and flatware reminded him of his grandmother's home. *I cannot believe that we will actually use these fancy dishes. At my grandmother's house, anything close to being this special is put away in her china cabinet. I would never even consider using any of it!*

Mr. J, sitting at his designated head of the table, was grinning while looking up at Bobby. "I hope your appetite is ready! My precious Ruby has prepared her famous lasagna for our dinner this evening!"

Bobby's eyes lit up like a child's on Christmas Day. "Lasagna?! That's my favorite dish!"

Mr. J howled with laughter. "I know, Bobby! If you haven't figured by now, I was sure to ask Eric about your favorite foods. That way, we would be prepared to serve you and to give you the best experience possible." Mr. J smiled as he looked at the startled expression on the young man's face. "Bobby, something I've learned over the years is that I always want to treat people as well, if not better than the way I'd like them to treat me. When you hold on to that principle, it will help to take you far in life."

At that moment, as Bobby took his seat, Mr. J's wife, Ruby, brought the hot lasagna dish over to the table and placed it between the garlic bread and salad. She looked at Bobby with a twinkle in her eye and said, "Now, look here, Bobby. Don't be shy. I want you to enjoy yourself. There's plenty here for you, so please dig in!"

Bobby grinned and said, "Yes, ma'am!"

As Ruby sat down, Mr. J placed his hands on the table and said, "Okay, I'm starving. Y'all mind if I say a blessing?"

"Go right ahead," Ruby responded. Bobby noticed the way that Mr. J and Ruby looked at each other. There was such a genuine love for one another, and he could see it in their eyes.

"Lord. Bless this food for the nourishment of our bodies. Amen!"

As they began to eat, Ruby asked Bobby, "So, what has been the highlight of your weekend?"

Bobby finished chewing his mouthful of delicious food before answering. He began to think back on all the experiences that he had visiting Mr. J's friends. *I've learned so much this weekend. How can I choose only one highlight?* "You know, each experience has been special in its way. I've learned a lot, and hopefully, the lessons will stay with me."

Mr. J wiped his mouth with his cloth napkin and said, "Bobby, the best way to remember is to put each lesson into practice at any given opportunity. You have to practice. And if you mess up, don't be too hard on yourself. Look at where you messed up, evaluate the experience, learn from it, and move on."

"You know, Mr. J, you make these things seem so simple," Bobby said.

Mr. J replied, "It's because I've come to realize that I'm where I am in life because of the grace of God, and what I've learned from the hundreds, maybe thousands of mistakes I've made. Even from the worst mistakes, I've always learned how to bounce back."

Uplifted by their conversation, the three of them continued to enjoy the delicious meal. After gratefully accepting a second helping of everything, Bobby sighed contently and leaned back in his chair.

"Now, I think it's time for dessert," Ruby declared, standing up and gathering plates.

Mr. J asked, "What's for dessert, love?"

Ruby looked at Bobby and asked, "How about vanilla bean ice cream on top of warm apple pie?"

A grinning Bobby responded, "Sounds good to me!"

Mr. J gave that all too familiar chuckle before saying, "Now, Bobby, there is one more story that I want you to hear while we eat our dessert. This story is the most special to me because it comes from the dearest person to me."

After Ruby placed the three dessert dishes on the table, she looked at Bobby with a warm smile and asked, "Bobby, are you ready to hear my story?"

Not knowing what to expect, Bobby smiled back and said, "Sure."

CHAPTER 17

Ruby was quiet while they all enjoyed dessert. Then she wiped her mouth with the napkin and gathered her thoughts. Ruby took a deep breath and turned to Bobby. "Let's see. Where do I begin? Okay, here we go. Now Bobby, brace yourself. I'm going to be very transparent because if there is one thing I've learned from my husband, transparency can help many people when shared the right way. So, here is my story.

"My childhood went by too fast. My parents divorced when I was four years old, so my older brother and I primarily grew up with our mom. As a young girl, I remember being in situations that no young girl should experience. I remember losing my virginity. I was fourteen, and the boy was nineteen. I wasn't willing or ready, and that experience had a serious impact on each of my decisions that followed. You know that seed that you and J talked about yesterday in our sitting room?"

Bobby nodded.

"Well, I believe that there was a seed planted in my mind that convinced me that I wasn't worth much more than for some guy's pleasure. Not long after that, my mom remarried. My stepfather, I couldn't stand that guy. He was so strict, and he would punish us for anything as simple as not refilling the ice tray. And then it happened. One day, he began to pay attention to me. I thought that he was paying attention to me like a father would pay attention to a daughter. He would take me out and talk about the different struggles that I was having with my mom. You know, daddy-daughter stuff. After a while, though, things began to get weird. He would do little things that were pretty uncomfortable, you know, things that would make you raise your eyebrows. He would touch me in inappropriate ways. I wanted to believe that it was accidental. Deep down, I knew that it was wrong."

"How old were you, Mrs. Ruby?" a curious Bobby asked.

"Oh, I was about fifteen at the time. And I wish I could say that it all stopped there. It didn't. My stepfather would sneak into my bedroom at night and do things to me that were not appropriate at all, especially from someone in a father's role. I got to the point where I firmly believed that my worth was my body, and my body was my worth. I became promiscuous. I'm not proud that I had allowed that seed to grow. I thought, 'Hmmm. I can get paid for doing what I'm doing.' Bobby, before I knew it, I was a prostitute."

Bobby's jaw dropped open. "Are you serious?" he asked. "You, a prostitute?" *I find that very hard to believe. She's such a virtuous woman. How could she have fallen into that type of lifestyle?* He had trouble wrapping his mind around the fact that this gentle yet dynamic older woman who exuded so much virtue and whose very presence brought a sense of peace could have possibly lived a prostitute's life.

"Yep, Bobby. Just like you've seen in the movies," Ruby said, shaking her head. "I dropped out of school, and that lifestyle took me to New York, where I lived for the next two years. And boy, I tell ya, that was a crazy life. I won't get into all the details; just know that I survived. I had dropped out of school, but I was no dummy. I guess you can say that some of my natural survival instincts kicked in to help me.

"Toward the end of my time there, I was dating a drug dealer. I remember getting in an argument with him and needing some space. Well, he thought that I was leaving him, so he got aggressive with me. He tried to stab me. Somehow, I was able to get my hand in front of my chest to block his knife, and I left with only a cut on my hand."

"Was he trying to kill you?" Bobby asked with genuine concern, and one eyebrow raised.

Ruby giggled and said, "He may have been, but guess what? I'm still here!"

Mr. J interrupted and said, "Yes, you are, sweetheart!"

Bobby watched the intimate way Mr. J and Mrs. Ruby's smiled at one another. *He is so comfortable with her telling this story. She just said to me that her drug dealer boyfriend tried to stab her while she was living the life of a prostitute, yet they're sitting here with such peace. Mr. J does not hold her former lifestyle against her. His lesson about damaged goods makes even more sense now because he's living it with his wife.*

Ruby beamed her smile on her husband and continued. "By this time, I had to figure out a way to get back home. To this day, I'm thankful for my family that helped me get home. Surprisingly, my mom allowed me back into her house. There were so many nights where I would reflect on my life while lying in my bed. I would think about the men who had abused me, the decisions that I had made, and my current state. And then, one night, it happened. I got a vision for my life. I began to remember the people who told me when I was younger that my life had value. I made a decision that I would no longer see myself as damaged goods. I wasn't sure where to start, so I figured that a good place would be to get around people who had a vision for their lives. Being around them helped me develop my vision, which led me to get a General Education Diploma. That was pretty easy, because like I told you earlier, I was no dummy. You see, even with a good head on my shoulders, I had lost track of my sense of purpose. After getting my GED, I went to the local community college. I felt like I had something to prove, so I was a top student. That led me to attend State University, which is where I met J."

Mr. J, winking at Bobby, interrupted again and said, "You see, she knew that I would be there. That's why she came to State!"

Ruby laughed heartily and said, "In your dreams, J!" Turning her smile to their guest, she continued. "Now Bobby, back to my story. That vision for my life led to things that I would never have imagined. I was a math major in college. I was involved with student organizations. I've gone on mission trips to South Africa, and they trusted me to lead some of them. I've had the opportunity to sing at so many places, from the school choir to political events, to professional sporting events. I ended up getting my Master's Degree and became a math professor at the local community college. And I have my J. You see, he sees me and loves me for me. He doesn't judge me by my past. He sees my worth, and he values and treasures me. He's helped me have more opportunities to share my story with people like you who may learn from my experiences. If I could leave you with one thought, Bobby, this is it: You don't have to allow your past to dictate your future." Ruby paused to let her words sink into Bobby's receptive mind. "Whenever you are being distracted by your past, just remember my story."

Speechless, Bobby looked at Mr. J, then at Ruby. He looked back at Mr. J, realizing that while Mr. J taught these principles, he also lived by them, to marry someone who had once seen herself as damaged goods. *Ruby's story is a powerful example of how a person's life can be transformed by watering the right seeds, by believing she is worthy of love and her life has value.* Bobby knew that it was time for him to head home, and at the same time, he was trying to digest what he'd just heard. He blurted out, "Mr. J, I can't thank you enough for everything. Your hospitality, the food, the lessons, everything."

Mr. J laughed and said, "No, Bobby. Thank you. Thank you for allowing me to serve you. Now, if you want to thank me, here is what you do. Be sure to apply each lesson learned. And like I said before, if you mess up, remember not to allow failure to be final. Get back up, learn from your mistakes, and keep going. Ruby and I are here for you if you need us. You can call us at any time."

"Thank you, Mr. J and Mrs. Ruby, for everything. And Mrs. Ruby, thank you for sharing your story of liberation with me. You brought to life so much of what Mr. J has been teaching me."

Bobby said his final goodbyes, grabbed the overnight bag that he had packed before dinner and got in his car, prepared for his one-hour drive home.

CHAPTER 18

After leaving Mr. J's home, Bobby was driving the speed limit while his mind was racing. It had begun to rain, and to the windshield wipers' rhythm, he replayed segments from the visits in his mind. From a better understanding of a seed's power to dealing with circumstances and the significance of a vision, Bobby felt fortified by wisdom to apply to his life for the better.

He was so thankful for the time that Mr. J had invested in him, although he felt overwhelmed. *Mr. J shared so many nuggets with me. And the people he introduced me to were utterly amazing. Mrs. Rogers and her resilience. Willie and his persistence. Ruby and her vision. Wow! What about me? Every one of the people I met was great. Am I able to overcome my upbringing and the words spoken over me? Do I have what it takes to overcome my past failures? Am I capable of ever having a story of overcoming obstacles as powerful as what those people experienced?*

When Bobby arrived safely home, it was dark, and he was grateful to park his car because he could see that the rain was changing to flurries when he looked up at the light shining through Eric's upstairs window. The Christmas season was upon them, and Bobby felt gratitude for his friend and his kindness to introduce him to Mr. J. *How can I thank Eric for being such a good friend?*

Bobby walked up the stairs to their apartment door, paused, and took a deep breath. He opened the door to see Eric sitting at the kitchen table with his headphones on and staring at the computer, wrapping up another successful night of business. Bobby pulled out a chair and sat at the table's opposite end.

Eric sat up straighter when he saw Bobby and pulled off his headphones, smiling. "There he is!" Eric exclaimed, pointing at Bobby. "So, how was your time with Mr. J?"

Bobby smiled too and said, "Trying to put everything into words would take the rest of this Christmas season."

As they both laughed, Eric noticed that something still seemed to be bothering his friend. Showing concern, Eric said, "I can tell that you took a lot of value from your time with Mr. J. And I know you well enough to recognize that something is still bothering you." After a brief pause, Eric politely asked, "Is there anything you would like to talk about?"

Without saying a word, Bobby clasped his hands and placed them on the table in front of him, looking down while twiddling his thumbs. *How can I share my true feelings with him? I'm thankful for everything, and my time this weekend was definitely life-changing. I don't want to come across as ungrateful. Well, I know that he cares, so I will share where I am at, from my heart.* After taking a moment to gather his thoughts, Bobby said, "Eric, I appreciate you introducing me to Mr. J, and I can't express to you how much the last couple of days have meant to me. He taught me so many valuable lessons that I will carry with me for the rest of my life. And the people who Mr. J introduced me to should each have a documentary of their own. I feel very encouraged. While I was driving home, though, the thought kept ringing in my mind, 'What about me? Am I capable of being persistent like Joe Rogers? Am I able to overcome circumstances like Ruby Owens? Am I able to overcome failures like Benny?' You see, Eric, I learned a lot over the weekend. Those stories of overcoming extreme odds were right for them. What about me?"

Eric paused before responding to Bobby. Reflecting on his time with Mr. J, Eric could hear that familiar, encouraging voice saying, "You don't always have to answer so quickly. Sometimes it's a good thing to take your time before responding." Eric, remembering those words, sat quietly. After another minute passed by, Eric spoke. "You know, Bobby, I'm glad you found value in your time with Mr. J because I was hoping you would get as much from him as I did."

Bobby nodded. Rather than judging Eric's words one by one as he had done just a couple of days ago, Bobby felt calm and filled with anticipation. By now, he realized that his friend had words of wisdom to offer.

"You know," Eric continued, "I also wrestled with some of the same thoughts that you just shared with me. I remember meeting Willie and his breathtaking accomplishment amazed me too. Do you want to know what I learned?"

"What's that?" asked Bobby.

Leaning forward, Eric looked Bobby in the eye and said, "I learned not to allow comparison to cripple my calling."

Bobby took his hands off the table, leaned back in his chair, and crossed his legs. He looked down and repeated to himself quietly, "Don't let comparison cripple my calling." After a moment, he looked at Eric and asked, "What does it mean not to allow comparison to cripple my calling?"

Eric smiled graciously at Bobby and responded. "Bobby, during our time together, Mr. J shared with me that everyone's life has a purpose. Unfortunately, not everyone discovers the purpose of their lives. However, some choose to find and pursue their purpose, and during their pursuit, they overcome incredible odds. They refuse to be enslaved by any obstacles that may have once overtaken them. Each person's pursuit of their purpose is unique. Your story of overcoming will be different than mine. And that's okay.

"So, in the pursuit of your life's purpose, don't get caught up in the details of other people's stories because their story is their story. And just like you're amazed at Mrs. Rogers' story, trust me when I say that she'll be amazed at yours. When you compare the details of your progress in your chapter two versus her progress in her chapter twelve, you risk the chance of becoming a slave to the comparison."

Eric paused as he reflected on his experience and then leaned forward, eager to explain. "Bobby, rather than comparing myself to anyone's amazing story of overcoming, I have learned to take principles of each lesson and apply them one by one in my life. I didn't pressure myself to change overnight. Little by little, I applied the principles, and before I knew it, I began to see success in my business and other areas of my life." Nodding with a smile, Eric said, "I'll give you the same advice Mr. J gave me. 'The best place for you to start is right where you are.'"

Bobby listened intently to every word that Eric said; it all made sense. He realized that he had been too hard on himself and was on his way to falling into the comparison trap. Like everything else that happened with Mr. J on the weekend, this conversation with Eric was right on time.

"Eric," Bobby said, his eyes bright, "I see what you're saying. I still have a question for you."

"Sure! Go ahead."

"I realize that I cannot do this on my own. I want to pursue my purpose, whatever that may be. And I do not want to fall into the trap of comparison. I'm willing to take baby steps along the way to my destiny. My question for you is, are you willing to help me?"

Eric smiled with a sense of relief and said to his friend, "Sure, Bobby. That's what friends are for."

Bobby laughed out loud and pointed across the room at his unfinished work project. "All right! Helping me finish this project will be a great start."

Eric laughed and agreed. Just like their days in college, they again began to work together. Only this time, Bobby had a clear purpose in mind. His start was strong, and working as a team with Eric, Bobby efficiently completed the project that evening. Smiling at his friend, Bobby took a deep breath and let it out, feeling liberated, grateful to be in a new chapter of his journey—a slave no more.

The End

ONE YEAR LATER

I t was Tuesday before Thanksgiving, and Bobby gathered his team around him in the company board room. He looked around the room and met each team member's eyes while describing the expectations for the holiday season upon them.

Confidently smiling, Bobby said, "I am so fortunate to have each of you as a part of my team. You are here for a reason, and I'm expecting the most productive and efficient season that our company has ever seen. I only expect it because I know that you are capable. Each of you is a star, so shine in your role. If you give your best, we will have great results. I believe in you."

The members of Bobby's team radiated a certain calm excitement that distinguished them in the distribution company. That energy all started with his leadership.

Bobby reflected on his life-altering weekend with Mr. J that happened almost a year earlier. That experience helped him return to work with a completely new mindset. The vice president of the company soon noticed the difference in Bobby's attitude, confidence, and production level. He chose to promote Bobby as a manager and placed him to lead a team of fifteen people.

One of the members, Anthony, spent considerable time observing Bobby. He watched the way Bobby conducted himself and was intrigued by how a young man in a leadership position could be so confident in his work, and at the same time, be so approachable.

After their team huddle, Anthony pulled Bobby aside. "Bobby, do you have a minute?"

"Sure, Anthony. For you, I can squeeze five minutes. Just walk with me."

As they walked together, Anthony noticed Bobby's genuine engagement with his team. No one seemed to be nervous because the manager was walking by; everyone seemed to be empowered by his presence.

Finding the courage to ask his question, Anthony took a deep breath and said, "Bobby, how did you do it?"

Bobby smiled and replied, "Anthony, what do you mean? How did I do what?"

Anthony took another deep breath as he gathered his thoughts. "It's like you are a completely different person from when you were in the manager's training program last year. You were not nearly as confident as you are now. I remember watching you from time to time, knowing that you were in training. I'm sure you were doing your job to the best of your ability, but you would get so easily frustrated. Now, I see you confident as a manager, respected by your team, and you easily complete your tasks. How did you do it?"

Bobby, reflecting on the lessons that he had been applying over the last year, smiled, stopped walking, and turned toward his younger co-worker. "Anthony, remind me. Did you play sports in college?"

"Yes, I played basketball."

"What position did you play?"

Anthony, wondering where Bobby was going with these questions, replied, "Point guard."

"Okay, I see. Now tell me this: Did you have coaches?"

Anthony laughed, knowing that Bobby already knew the answer, and said, "Come on, man. Of course, we had coaches. We had our head coach, assistant coaches, and we also had our position coaches."

"Okay. Just making sure you're on your toes!" Bobby said with a chuckle. He could tell that he was setting Anthony at ease. "I had coaches during my football career like you had coaches during your basketball career. Last year, I learned the importance of having a good coach in life. The rest of our lives is much longer than the four years we played ball in college. It dawned on me that if having a good coach is important for me to be successful in sports, then how much more important is it for me to have a coach or mentor in life? You mentioned you had a position coach, right?"

Anthony nodded. "Yes."

"So, the position coach knew the ins and out of how to play your position, point guard. He probably played that very same role during his career. Does that sound about right?"

Anthony nodded again and said, "Yes."

"About a year ago, I realized that I needed a coach in life, someone like the coach you had who knew your position and knew it well. I needed a mentor. It was important to have someone who could help me look at where I was in life and guide me in the right direction. And thankfully, that was when my roommate helped connect me with the right person. My mentor helped me understand the impact of discouraging thoughts dominating me and the benefit of changing my mindset. With his guidance and practical lessons of overcoming, I was able to move on to a brighter future."

"Wow," an intrigued Anthony replied, "that's amazing."

Bobby laughed and said, "Well, having Mr. J as a mentor has been life-changing. And along with having him in my life, two additional factors have been beneficial. One, I had to apply what he taught. And two, I agreed to allow my roommate to hold me accountable. You see, I realized the value of having a teammate, and it works just like you playing basketball. You knew that your performance affected the overall team's performance. In my case, my roommate is a teammate in life. He's pursuing his goals, and I'm pursuing my goals. And along the way, we're encouraging each other to give our very best. If one of us ever feels discouraged, the other can be an encouragement. There have been times when my roommate has had to remind me of the lessons I learned. And you know what? I welcome the reminders because I am grateful for the proof that he's keeping each lesson in front of me. Our teamwork has allowed me to be where I am today."

Anthony, looking thoughtful, was silent a moment, listening to the swirl of enthusiastic voices around him and Bobby where they stood by the main office's open door. Remarking on what Bobby had shared with him, Anthony said, "Everything you just told me makes total sense, and I would love to have a similar experience. Only, I'm not sure where to start." With a hopeful smile, he continued. "If it's not out of line to ask, do you know anyone who would be willing to mentor me?"

Bobby smiled and started walking. Delighted by Anthony's questions, Bobby gestured to the young man to follow him. "Come on, Anthony. Let's go to my office." Anthony laughed, offering Bobby a high-five, and they slapped palms while walking together. Bobby, already enjoying his turn to be a mentor, added, "I may have a couple of ideas."

KEY POINTS

Chapter 1

- Don't allow other people's thoughts about you or your abilities to hinder you from tapping into your potential.
- Your past does not predetermine your future.
- It's okay to talk out a problem with a friend who knows you and cares.

Chapter 2

- As a friend helping a friend, it is important to establish common ground. Showing an ability to relate allows your friend to trust your words.
- It's okay to air out your thoughts to yourself while finding a way to ask for help, ask questions, and receive guidance.

Chapter 3

- To be a slave means to be completely subservient to a dominant influence.

- We can be a slave to past failures or circumstances, which can lead to limited thinking.
- While we cannot control our past circumstances, allowing ourselves to continue to be dominated by limited thinking is a choice.
- Identifying a strong desire is the first step to break free from limited thinking.
- A mentor is valuable in all areas of life and can help guide you to move from being dominated by your past to living a victorious life.
- A mentor sees the good qualities in you and can help you learn to turn those qualities into strengths.
- Living a life of victory begins with a strong desire, and having someone help guide you.
- It is crucial to apply the mentor's guidance like a roadmap, and following it can help lead you to your desired destination and beyond.
- Associating with individuals who live lives of victory will inspire you to be better and see yourself in a better light.

Chapter 4

- Breaking free from limited thinking may require doing something out of the ordinary.
- There are people in places who are willing to help you, and receiving their guidance may require you to sacrifice and step outside of your comfort zone.

- It is essential to have an open mind and heart when spending time with a mentor who has achieved what you are looking to achieve.

Chapter 5

- Find a way to help people, and do it with a cheerful heart. Treat their interests as if they're your own. When you see them making progress toward their goals, celebrate with them as if it is your own success.
- Find a mentor who has what you are looking for, and when they speak, treat their words as precious as pure gold.

Chapter 6

- Your story is your story. The lens from which you choose to view your story determines the value that you receive from it.
- There is always a root that leads to an action. Consider that when dealing with people, you are often also dealing with the influence of their background.
- Every seed bears fruit. The care taken for the seed determines the type of fruit that it produces.
- Your mind is like soil with seeds have been planted throughout your life.
- Any word said about you, whether positive or negative, is like a "You are." When you accept the "You are" words that are said to you, they become,

"I am," which are the most important words you can say to yourself.

- What you believe is what you become. When you accept the "You are" words, you allow the planting of a seed. With the planted seed, your choice then becomes to either nourish the seed to grow, or starve the seed so that it eventually dies.

- Words spoken over you have been positive or negative seeds, which have led to your positive or negative thoughts. It is up to you to choose which seeds to nourish so that they flourish and which seeds to starve to make their impact minimal.

Chapter 7

- When facing a challenging situation, the first step to overcoming is making up your mind that you will succeed. The odds may be stacked against you, there may be some bumps on the road, and others around you in a similar situation may give up. Choose to persevere, and you will ensure that you are on the right track.

- If you fall, be sure to fall forward. That way, at least you're falling in the right direction.

- Being the first in your family to experience success in any given field will come with challenges. There will be discouraging voices around you. Stay the course, and know that there is satisfaction in choosing to be victorious over circumstances.

Chapter 8

- There is power in identifying a vision for your life, so find even a small, attainable goal. While in pursuing your goal, you may stumble across your long-term life goal, which will help guide you as long as you keep it in front of you.

- Do not feel guilty for wanting more out of life. There is nothing wrong with wanting more from life than what those who came before you have achieved. Allow their ceiling to be your floor. Know that you are setting a higher ceiling for those who will come after you.

- While in pursuit of your vision, do not be surprised when you face trials. It is up to you to decide how you view each circumstance. You can either allow it to keep you from reaching your goal. Or you can view it as a hurdle that is helping you to develop more perseverance.

- Amid hardship, keep moving toward your goal.

- It's okay to ask for help and receive help.

- When you have a strong vision, you will find a way to get where you need to go. Make up your mind, and don't allow dream-snatchers to hinder you. Understand that dream-snatchers can be enemies, and they can also be loved ones who want their best for you. That is why it is crucial to develop a strong vision and know why you are doing what you're doing. Please keep it in front of you so that no one can deter you from your set path.

Chapter 9

- While in pursuit of your vision, there will be voices all around you. They may be the voices of colleagues, or they may be the words from your childhood that have followed you for years. It's up to you to determine which voices you allow to influence you.

- When it is your time to be promoted, be careful not to allow the limiting voices from the past or your present environment to discourage you from tapping into your potential. Those voices may remind you of your past failures or circumstances. However, you must resolve to keep your vision in front of you and maximize the life speaking voices that encourage you to press toward your goal.

- Each limiting voice and obstacle present in a given situation is an opportunity to overcome. When you overcome, hold on to the feeling of victory. Know that your strength is developing and that each success is bringing you one step closer to attaining your vision. It is your choice how you view each obstacle: as a hindrance or as an opportunity.

- Be careful of feeling sorry for yourself. Although your past circumstances are your legitimate life experiences, feeling sorry for yourself for too long will hold you bound. Take the proper steps to deal with your traumatic experiences, whether sharing with a counselor or a mentor. Then, keeping your vision in front of you, allow your past challenges to serve as a motivating force.

- Surround yourself with people who will help you attain your vision. Hold on to the good things that they say about you, and let their positive voices drown out the limiting voices from your past. Allow their life speaking words to fuel you as you progress toward your vision.

- Take time, in gratitude, to reflect on your progress. Know that your victories will inspire others that they are capable of breaking free from the limiting voices from their past.

Chapter 10

- Work hard at the task at hand. Pursue excellence, and keep a good attitude. The right people will eventually take notice.

- Develop a clear vision and keep it in front of you. Be clear on your goal and find ways to keep your vision fresh.

- Ultimately, to move from limited thinking to achieving a life vision will require sacrifices. Be willing to do what it takes.

- Once you have your vision, develop a plan to help you get there, and stay focused. Have a friend in your corner who will help cheer you on to your goals.

Chapter 11

- Whenever learning a lesson from any kind of testimonial—whether written or oral—take time to reflect.

- It is up to you what you choose to do with your thoughts, positive or not so positive, shaped by your experiences.

- Bad seeds or thoughts that come from bad experiences or negative words spoken over you are like a spark that can cause a destructive fire in your life. You decide how to handle it. Do you fan the flames of the damaging thoughts by repeating them to yourself and associating with people who hold the same belief? Or do you choose to extinguish the flame by saying the opposite? Combat the harmful words and experiences with reaffirming words about yourself, like "There is a divine purpose for my life, and I will use the challenges from my past to propel me forward."

- Your life has value, and there is a significant purpose for your life. Believe and affirm this truth, and surround yourself with people who help to nourish this seed of truth.

- Everyone has positive and negative experiences that have happened to this point in their lives. If you only focus on the adverse experiences, it is like being enslaved to your past. You will benefit by going through a proper evaluation process for each harmful experience by speaking with a mentor or counselor. However, your response to those situations is your choice. When you choose to evaluate and learn from each experience, they can become your driving force toward a life of freedom and position you to help others.

Chapter 12

- A strong vision can keep you from making the same mistakes as those who came before you. If there is a trend in your family that you do not want to repeat, keep the vision of what you desire in front of you, and have people in your life who are successful in that given area who are willing to hold you accountable and help keep you on track.

- You will find that, more than likely, breaking a family trend is not easy. It takes a strong vision, focus, and a friend to help you change your family's course. If you find yourself getting off track, don't be too hard on yourself. Refocus, and get back on track. Remember, you are looking to shift a generational trend. Providing a better life for your children will have its bumps along the way, so always remember to stay the course.

- Realize that you are not alone. Others around you come from similar backgrounds and have found success in changing the course of their family's destiny.

- In successful relationships, individuals play different roles. Rather than being frustrated with your differences, find ways where your strengths complement each other and become a better team.

- Keeping your vision in front of you and staying the course will have a generational impact on your family, so be encouraged to press through the challenging times knowing that you are changing the course of your family's history.

Chapter 13

- Every person has value. It's up to you to decide whether to judge someone by their outward appearance, or see their worth inside.
- Whether you feel that your life has been damaged by poor decisions you've made, negative experiences, or from a physical ailment, it is up to you to decide whether to accept the designation of the scars as your final destiny.
- Be careful not to devalue your life based on your past experiences.
- Move on from seeing your life as damaged goods and learn to find the value that your life still holds. The scars from your past do not determine the value of your life.

Chapter 14

- While serving as a mentor, be attentive because there are lessons for you to learn through the experience with your mentee.

- Every situation presents an opportunity to learn, and it is crucial to have the awareness to pick up the subtleties within each experience.
- Don't allow life's circumstances to determine your destiny.

Chapter 15

- Use setbacks as an opportunity to reflect on and evaluate your situation.
- Learn to focus on what you have rather than what you lack. Be resourceful. There are always hidden treasures in front of you and within you. It takes a particular awareness to find them.
- When going through a test in life, lean on your support system. It is better to walk through the trial with someone by your side than attempt to handle it all on your own.
- When faced with a trial—handicap, negative experience, or any unfortunate situation—it is up to you to decide how to respond. Will you focus on the circumstance and the impact that it has had on your life, or will you find the opportunities and ways to overcome it despite your situation? Will you be a victim, or will you find the victory? Choose to focus on opportunities, knowing that each victory over a trial provides a lifelong gift for yourself that you can also share with others.
- Take a thorough evaluation of yourself. In every circumstance, evaluate where you can improve. It

is also a good practice to ask someone who has your best interest at heart to help you assess your situation and see where you can find areas of opportunity.

- You are capable. Keep your vision in front of you, and allow it to override your challenges. There will be positive and negative voices around you. Choose to listen to the encouraging voices. Let them support you as you walk toward your vision.

- Learn to evaluate a situation and make decisions that best suit your strengths. Make the best decision to help you overcome your circumstance, knowing that your path is different from that of another.

Chapter 16

- When serving as a mentor, put your best foot forward. Go above and beyond to serve your mentee. In this way, you show them their value and the significance of serving others, and by modeling a servant's heart, they will know how to treat others when they enter a mentor's role.

- Treat people as well and even better than how you'd like others to treat you.

- A great way to remember life lessons is to put what you have learned into practice at every given opportunity. It takes practice for the lessons you learn to become your lifestyle. If you mess up, don't be too hard on yourself. Evaluate the experience, learn from it, and move on.

- Every time you bounce back from a mistake, you have another experience under your belt to evaluate and learn from that will help you get closer to who you envision yourself becoming.

Chapter 17

- Be careful of which seeds in your life you allow to take root and grow.
- Don't judge a book by its cover. You never know the trials that a person has gone through.
- If you're struggling to see your life beyond the mistakes you've made, get around people who have a good vision for their lives. Associating with them will help you develop a vision for your own life.
- Begin with a decision to move beyond seeing your life as damaged goods. Surround yourself with people who will help you hold fast to your commitment.
- Take baby steps toward your vision. When recovering from mistakes or life failures, celebrate the small victories. While they may seem insignificant, don't underestimate their role in helping you achieve your purpose.
- Developing your vision and taking steps to achieve your goal can lead to success beyond your imagination.

- Living a life of victory after experiencing failure stems from not allowing your past to dictate your future. Your life is valuable; keep your vision ahead of you and your history where it is: in the past.

- If you mess up, don't allow failure to be final. Get back up, learn from your mistakes, and keep moving toward your vision.

Chapter 18

- When a friend comes to you for support, remember that it is good to take your time before responding. This pause shows them that you are genuinely listening.

- Do not allow comparison with others to cripple you from achieving your vision. Each person's pursuit of their purpose is unique. Your story of overcoming will be different than the next person's.

- Don't get caught up in the details of other people's journey. Just as you may be amazed at other people's stories of overcoming, there will be people who are similarly surprised by your story. Be cautious of comparing your story in its infancy to someone's story further along.

- Take each principle learned, and apply them one by one. Don't put pressure on yourself to change overnight. The best place to start is right where you are today.

About the Author

Paul A. Henderson is a sports chaplain, author, and motivational speaker. He is a former track and field athlete at Virginia Commonwealth University. Paul blogs at Fatherhood on the Fly, where his slogan is, "We're learning, we're growing, and we're getting better one day at a time."

Author portrait by
DeAudrea 'Sha' Rich

Using a combination of encouragement and humor from daily experiences with his boys, Paul inspires dads from all backgrounds to embrace the journey of fatherhood and everything that comes with it.

In Richmond, Virginia, U.S.A., Paul is a husband to his wife, Kierra, of Beloved Mama. Together they love their four sons—PJ, Joey, David, and Noah.

www.paulanthonyhenderson.com

Facebook Page
@Fatherhood0nTheFly

Instagram
@fatherhood_onthefly

A free ebook edition is available with the purchase of this book.

To claim your free ebook edition:

1. Visit MorganJamesBOGO.com
2. Sign your name CLEARLY in the space
3. Complete the form and submit a photo of the entire copyright page
4. You or your friend can download the ebook to your preferred device

Print & Digital Together Forever.

Snap a photo   Free ebook   Read anywhere